COMPLETE
QUARTERBACKING

COMPLETE QUARTERBACKING

Don Read

Human Kinetics

Library of Congress Cataloging-in-Publication Data

Read, Don, 1933-
 Complete quarterbacking / Don Read.
  p. cm.
 ISBN 0-7360-3984-8 (Soft cover)
 1. Quarterback (Football) 2. Football--Coaching. I. Title.
 GV951.3 .R43 2002
 796.33'2--dc21

                                                        2002001756

ISBN: 0-7360-3984-8

Copyright © 2002 by Don Read

All rights reserved. Except for use in a review, the reproduction or utilization of this work in any form or by any electronic, mechanical, or other means, now known or hereafter invented, including xerography, photocopying, and recording, and in any information storage and retrieval system, is forbidden without the written permission of the publisher.

Acquisitions Editor: Todd Jensen
Developmental Editor: Cynthia McEntire
Assistant Editor: John Wentworth
Copyeditor: Erin Cler
Proofreader: Coree Schutter
Graphic Designer: Nancy Rasmus
Graphic Artist: Francine Hamerski
Photo Manager: Leslie A. Woodrum
Cover Designer: Jack W. Davis
Photographer (cover): © Al Tielemans/SI/Newsport
Photographer (interior): Larry Bates unless otherwise noted
Art Manager: Carl D. Johnson
Illustrator: Roberto Sabas
Printer: Versa Press

Human Kinetics books are available at special discounts for bulk purchase. Special editions or book excerpts can also be created to specification. For details, contact the Special Sales Manager at Human Kinetics.

Printed in the United States of America   10 9 8 7 6 5 4 3 2 1

Human Kinetics

Web site: www.HumanKinetics.com

United States: Human Kinetics
P.O. Box 5076
Champaign, IL 61825-5076
800-747-4457
e-mail: humank@hkusa.com

Canada: Human Kinetics
475 Devonshire Road Unit 100
Windsor, ON N8Y 2L5
800-465-7301 (in Canada only)
e-mail: orders@hkcanada.com

Europe: Human Kinetics
107 Bradford Road
Stanningley
Leeds LS28 6AT, United Kingdom

+44 (0) 113 255 5665
e-mail: hk@hkeurope.com

Australia: Human Kinetics
57A Price Avenue
Lower Mitcham, South Australia 5062
08 8277 1555
e-mail: liahka@senet.com.au

New Zealand: Human Kinetics
P.O. Box 105-231, Auckland Central
09-523-3462
e-mail: hkp@ihug.co.nz

For my mother, Emily Read, who gave me life, direction, and love; Lois, my wife of 40 years, who shared my life and allowed me to share hers; and my daughter Beth and son Bruce, of whom I am most proud

Contents

Foreword

The game of football is not only the most popular sport in our society today, it is the greatest team sport of all time. The most demanding, thrilling, and rewarding position in football is quarterback. Of course, I write that with just a tad bit of bias having played only quarterback for two years in Pop Warner, four years in high school, four years in college, and 15 years in the National Football League.

During that 25-year span, I had many coaches—some good, some great, some so-so, and some not so wonderful. But through it all, I learned about not only being a better quarterback but being a better teammate and better person in general. My time spent with Don Read was special to me because he helped me become all three.

There are few coaches who are more knowledgeable about playing and coaching quarterbacks than Don Read. His background, experience, and success contribute to making this book a must for anyone who wants to play quarterback or coach the position. The detail and breadth, the compassion and understanding, and the positive and exciting manner with which Don communicates take me right back to our quarterback meetings of 30 years ago.

Few bonds are as strong as the bonds between teacher and pupil or coach and player. When that relationship blossoms into a friendship forged on the gridiron, you have something unique and special. One of the many things I appreciate about Don Read is how he has always kept in touch over the years. Nary a season has passed without an epistle full of encouragement and inspiration from the "old coach."

As challenging as it is to play quarterback, coaching the position is just as tough. *Complete Quarterbacking* will provide a blueprint for success. It is about becoming a winner, and it was written by a winner.

Dan Fouts

Acknowledgments

Two people head up my list of those who contributed immensely to this writing project. First and foremost, thanks to my bright and talented wife, Lois, who wore out two computers keeping my act together with respect to this book! Another debt of gratitude goes to Jeff Ketron, the most capable head football coach at Douglas County High School, Colorado. Jeff is solely responsible for the excellent charts and graphs and provided solid ideas for this manuscript.

The job done here is deserving of the great influence that I received from so many comrades in arms over the years, some of whom are the best in the business. I salute them, thank them, and dedicate this book to them. These friends and fellow coaches served with me at six different locales. The following names are presented with gratitude and for posterity:

Dick Arbuckle	Craig Howard	Myron Ringstad
Bob Beers	Tommy Lee	Jack Roach
Carl Blackburn	Roy Love	Sam Robertson
Jessie Branch	Ralph MacPhever	Phil Ryan
Claude Brock	John Marshall	Joe Schaffeld
Fred Brock	Dale McGriff	Paul Sherbina
Doug Camilli	Bill Moos	Bill Smith
Ross Carriaga	Howard Morris	Steve Sogge
Len Casanova	Scott Nelson	Jerome Sours
Vic Clark	Ted Ogdahl	Skip Stahley
Gene Dahlquist	Buzz Ostrom	Frank St. Peter
Don Deise	Kraig Paulson	Dave Stromswold
Mick Dennehy	Brent Pease	Jim Underhill
George Dyer	Robin Pflugrad	Bud VanDeren
Dick Enright	Bruce Read	Fred Von Appen
Gary Hamlet	Dick Read	Joe Wade
Bob Hamilton	Len Read	George Weeks
Bill Hammer	Dave Reeves	Len Younce

Introduction

The gridiron is like a battlefield. The position players are the soldiers, and the quarterback is the field general. *Complete Quarterbacking* contains both new insights and old established doctrine toward developing and encouraging winning performances by the quarterback. In analyzing this unique position, a degree of bias and opinion is mixed with proved absolutes. There is great need in today's football arena for this book; little in-depth information exists in print on the scope of modern quarterback play.

Clearly, the road to being a successful quarterback is not easy, nor is it for everyone. This fact is gospel and should be understood by all concerned. The challenges presented by the position appear never ending and often seem insurmountable. Compare the task of quarterbacking a successful offense to driving a car; to operate effectively, *all* contributing components have to function correctly and in a timely manner. For the quarterback, the word "all" refers to the overwhelming physical and mental demands required by the position.

Many facets go into making a successful quarterback. My passion for the game and 40 years' experience have led me to isolate the most desired and important aspects of quarterbacking. The information in the chapters ahead will serve as a guide and resource to those wanting to master playing quarterback or coaching quarterbacks, or who want to better appreciate quarterback play.

Complete Quarterbacking offers a nucleus of essential quarterback core material. Digestion of the content and application of these principles, sometimes referred to as pearls of wisdom, will help both the novice and the veteran signal caller.

There are multiple reasons for reading this book. You will become better informed as a player, coach, or fan of the role the quarterback plays on a successful team. Your quarterback sense will be scrutinized, intensified, refined, and broadened. You will learn to appreciate the quarterback's role on the team. *Complete Quarterbacking* was intended to go beyond the how of playing quarterback to the why, when, and where, which are important elements in the big picture of what this position encompasses.

Precise methodology is stressed throughout. A cup of philosophy and a spoonful of theory are sprinkled in to reinforce the scope of the quarterback's play. Thus, what's contained in this book is a recipe for success. Drills, photos, and illustrations provide clear application of the principles discussed in the text, presenting the necessary visual adaptation for understanding the concepts.

Being a good quarterback requires know-how for execution. To be a great field general, it also is necessary to understand the why and when to do what. These decision-making aspects of execution are an integral part of quarterbacking. In the chapters that follow, you will find an enthusiastic presentation of the entire gamut of quarterbacking, including the physical and mental demands.

The information is presented clearly and simply, with photos, illustrations, and examples from real game situations. Each chapter covers a specific phase of quarterbacking, from quarterback fundamentals in the running and passing games to the techniques required for successful play calling. Game preparation, evaluation, and year-round training are analyzed.

Development of a signal caller takes many paths. The best route is one that takes into account the quarterback's natural skills, the coach's offensive philosophy, and the nature of the team. The kind of offense, coaching style, and amount of time spent on refining the skills involved will, in the end, mold the quarterback into whatever he and his offense are to be. And let's not forget to add to this formula a necessary good measure of athletic ability, so critical for execution.

Any improvement that takes place depends on countless considerations but mostly on a positive, relentless, constructive effort, especially for a quarterback seeking to conquer the basic fundamentals necessary to effectively perform. The primary thrust of this book, therefore, is to examine the detailed elements of a quarterback's skills and how they are interwoven with those of his teammates.

It is my intention, as well as my hope, that by studying this book you will gain a new perspective to a complex position. When you have absorbed the final page, more than anything else I trust you will feel that your time was well spent. Then and only then can I feel rewarded for my efforts, allowing this endeavor to become a win–win project for both of us.

Key to Diagrams

W	Weakside linebacker
DE	Defensive end
T	Tackle
M	Middle linebacker
S	Strongside linebacker, safety
N	Nose tackle
OLB	Outside linebacker
ILB	Inside linebacker
SS	Strong safety
FS	Free safety
C	Corner (defense), center (offense)
C	Defensive key for quarterback
WR	Wide receiver
TE	Tight end
RB	Running back
G	Guard
⬮	Quarterback
⊕	Center
⊤	Blocking route
↑	Running route
⚡	Handoff
⋮	Pass
▼	Drop linebacker
Z	Z-route receiver
LOS	Line of scrimmage
⟋	Blocking angle on offensive player

CHAPTER 1

PROFILE OF A SUCCESSFUL QUARTERBACK

John Robinson, the former head coach of USC, UNLV, and the Los Angeles Rams, once said of a quarterback, "He will for sure drive the nicest car and date the prettiest girl." This may or may not always be true, but without a doubt today's quarterback plays the biggest role in any offense regardless of the system of play. The cold, hard fact is that the more talented the quarterback, the better the offense operates. Teams find it difficult to win without a capable quarterback; for some teams, it's almost impossible.

The quarterback is a combination of a point guard in basketball and a pitcher in baseball. He is the mental blend of a chess player, big-game hunter, and hockey goalie. Believing in himself establishes confidence and confidence leads to escalated performance. Believing establishes the self-esteem needed to do whatever job has to be done.

It is not difficult to lose or be an average quarterback. Failure is in one way or another self-inflicted. All you have to do is nothing. Winning takes preparation, effort, and leadership, which starts with the quarterback. The bigger the influence he has on those around him, the greater the chance for victory. He can be, and most of the time is, the difference between a successful program and an unsuccessful one.

The quarterback is more than special. He is the man, the cement in the concrete, the guy out front, and the coach on the field. The field general is the take-charge player, the final word on the gridiron, and he needs to be his team's mentor. There is no other position in football that is as demanding or as complicated and important to a team than the quarterback. The guy who lines up behind the center sets the tone and dynamics for every play attempt. John F. Kennedy once said, "To whom much is given, much is required." This statement says it all with respect to playing quarterback.

A quarterback's mental qualities often will determine how successful he is, but his physical characteristics are also important. Many players cannot play quarterback because they don't possess the physical makeup to handle the punishment the position attracts. Weight training and a proper diet are allies to any quarterback. Injuries often are directly related to lack of physical stature.

Playing quarterback is not for everyone. No position requires more physical toughness. On an average NFL roster, you will find a depth chart indicating a list of three deep at quarterback. All other positions show a two- or two-and-a-half-deep roster. It's difficult to stay healthy playing this position. A quarterback is every opponent's target.

In football, the range of comprehensive demands is enormous. The quarterback's responsibilities overlap all other positions and have much to do with how other players perform their jobs. The mental aspects of quarterbacking require, above all else, perception and instinct. Learning the quarterback position is a continual, intense process.

There are few shortcuts to being a quarterback because the position itself requires constant adjustments. There is an ongoing urgency that asks for excellence and know-how. Being a field general requires patience and understanding to produce the final product necessary to compete in each game.

Be they physical or mental, the expectations for a quarterback are somewhat overpowering. He is either the problem or the solution to the needs of his team. He will provide the most impact during the 48 or 60 minutes of play each game, depending on the degree of his preparation and physical makeup. This absolute is what quarterbacking is all about.

Quarterbacks come in many shapes and sizes, but ability and know-how generally determine how successfully they perform. Some can run fast; others are big, and the variety of athletic skills they exhibit make each unique in his own way. Still, why is the quarterback so important? The quarterback has to wear many different hats to meet high expectations, both physically and mentally. His makeup and ability are at the heart of every team.

Profiling a 21st-century quarterback is complex; the scope and depth of what he is asked to do are mind-boggling, particularly when we realize that high school quarterbacks are teenagers and college signal callers are not much older. To be effective these days, a quarterback must master countless physical skills and at the same time possess a solid understanding of the game. This being so, quarterbacking is difficult, and few excel to dominance at playing the position. With this in mind, let us explore what is involved in playing this prestigious, though challenging, position.

© Newsport Photography

■ A successful quarterback is physically strong and mentally confident. Brett Favre of the Packers is a good example of a consistent quarterback with a strong arm who is able to lead his team.

Mental Factors

A successful quarterback exhibits both strong physical traits and solid mental preparation. The mental aspects of the position are the intangibles that usually set quarterbacks apart from one another and their teammates. Here are the major mental elements a quarterback in today's game needs to exhibit if he is to be effective:

- Football savvy. Today's quarterback needs to know the game inside and out. He needs to have complete knowledge of all things pertaining to the position, both technical and theoretical.

- Mental toughness. Today's quarterback needs to have the ability to handle the pressure created by the game itself and the circumstances in which the game evolves.

- Poise. He must be able to summon up a feeling of calm when the surrounding situation is chaotic. His control influences not only himself but his teammates as well.

- Perception and anticipation. The quarterback must be able to predetermine situations and take advantage of given opportunities.

- Confidence. The quarterback must believe strongly in himself, the system, and his supporting cast. He must feel that the unexpected can be accomplished.

- Self-discipline. He must be willing to commit time and energy to developing his skills to get the job done. He also must be able to focus on the job at hand.

- Competitiveness. He must possess a burning desire to be the best and compete all out to win in any situation.

- Leadership. He must be able to inspire others to perform at their maximum abilities.

All of these traits and the degree to which a quarterback possesses them are most often what separates successful quarterbacks from unsuccessful quarterbacks. Everyone wants to win; winning requires quality performance. Many quarterbacks play and compete vigorously, but they never reach their potential. There are three general reasons for this. First, some quarterbacks underestimate what they are capable of doing. Second, sometimes their coaches haven't pushed them hard enough or provided the proper expertise to be forceful players. Third, simply too many are mentally or physically lazy. A few don't set their goals high enough or project the objectives they need to achieve excellence and master the position.

Quarterbacks have to understand the importance of goal setting if they want to be at the top of their form. Quarterbacks blessed with an extra measure of ability need to be told privately to set extra-high goals for themselves. For the most part, an athlete's limits are in his mind. Therefore, the biggest barrier to achieving more resides mainly within the athlete. The coach's role should be to provide the coaching and encouragement necessary to help the athlete reach his lofty objectives. In the final analysis, the quarterback himself will have the most responsibility for how good he becomes.

A quarterback who possesses an ample share of competitiveness, self-discipline, confidence, mental toughness, and football savvy will be successful—that is the bottom line. The field general who lacks any or all of these qualities has a much more difficult quest. There are a lot more quarterbacks who lack these skills than those who have the complete package. Only through intense work can those possessing fewer of these skills overcome and excel.

One measuring device a quarterback can use is to compare some of his mental traits with those of other quarterbacks who are playing today or who have recently played. Self-assessment is healthy and motivational. (See the quarterback percentage profile chart, figure 1.1.) The percentages will change when the level of competition increases or decreases. The type of offense and the quality of personnel involved also affect the comparison.

The assets a quarterback possesses and the degree to which he possesses them vary depending on the setting. Setting refers to a wide range of criteria, including offensive philosophy, level of play, ability of teammates, and type of defense used by the opponent. In general, the percentages presented are a reasonable assumption when looking at the large number of people playing this position.

The criteria chart shown in figure 1.1 is constantly redefined by the rules of the game, experience of the team, the quarterback's attitude, and the coaching philosophy. Every quarterback is unique, and how he plays the position becomes his personal trademark.

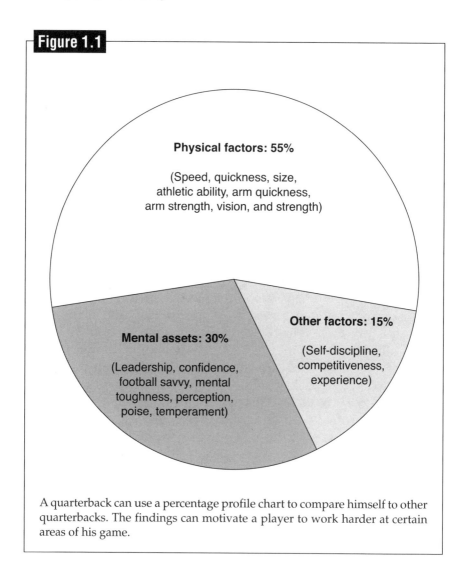

Figure 1.1

Physical factors: 55%

(Speed, quickness, size,
athletic ability, arm quickness,
arm strength, vision, and strength)

Other factors: 15%

(Self-discipline,
competitiveness,
experience)

Mental assets: 30%

(Leadership, confidence,
football savvy, mental
toughness, perception,
poise, temperament)

A quarterback can use a percentage profile chart to compare himself to other quarterbacks. The findings can motivate a player to work harder at certain areas of his game.

Spark

Spark is a mental intangible that the quarterback draws from to influence his teammates' performances, pushing them to play at a level above their norm. Spark is paramount in the success of a quarterback. A quarterback with spark can ignite his teammates' drive and direction. The quarterback doesn't have to be the type of player who always hollers and cheers, but he must be respected and looked up to by the other players.

Being positive, optimistic, and competitive is an aspect of a quarterback's personality, and he must be genuine and continuously illustrate these qualities to his teammates. He has to care about his comrades, as well as believe that they can get their jobs done. A quarterback should let each player know of his faith in him and the fact that supporting him is an ongoing process.

To be effective, the signal caller has to show proper habits and dedication toward excellence. His willingness to spend extra time developing himself and others often will trigger the commitment to win on the part of the entire team. Great quarterbacks are a combination of many things, but first they are good people. Make no mistake, the personality of the team is a direct reflection of how the quarterback thinks and acts.

Courtesy of Don Read

■ A quarterback's competitiveness is a vital contribution to the success of his team.

Leadership

An integral part of playing quarterback is leadership. Because leading takes many forms, there is no absolute blueprint for its installation or existence. Some components of leadership specific to quarterbacking merit examination.

All successful leaders are good managers of people and information. Their approach and manner may be radically different, but approach is not the most important thing. Accomplishment in leading is a process. A leader must be able to demonstrate different personality traits at appropriate times and places and in different situations.

All good leaders possess these 10 common factors:

1. Ability to perceive, digest, and deal with many different personalities.
2. Ability to give appropriate guidance to those around him.
3. Ability to handle the pressure of any given situation.
4. Mastery of self-sacrifice for the good of others.
5. Awareness of morale, harmony, and optimism of the team.
6. Ability to think positively in a negative environment.
7. Drive to be first in all endeavors requiring commitment to established goals.
8. Mastery of effective communication skills and the desire to continually develop them.
9. Desire to go out of his way to motivate others.
10. Knowledge of the strengths and weaknesses of all aspects of the system of play, personnel, and program philosophy.

These 10 principles are the foundation for quality leadership. Some quarterbacks have more of these than others. A leader can use many methods to get effective results from those he leads. Approaches to leadership range in style from the tough, strong, noncompromising person to the soft-spoken, interacting, hands-on guy.

Two contrasting giants from the world of politics who illustrate the point of leaders with diversified styles are Theodore Roosevelt and Abraham Lincoln. Roosevelt demonstrated an authoritarian, dynamic, vociferous personality. Lincoln often said "we" and had deep convictions for those he led and served.

Some of the most proven leaders in football were masters at communication and leadership. Heading the list is former Los Angeles Ram Norm Van Brocklin, who was said to be extremely direct and challenging to his team. Johnny Unitas of the Baltimore Colts was able to ignite others with the spark in his eyes. The San Francisco 49ers have had many great quarterbacks, but Joe Montana led his 49er teams with what has been described as visible confidence.

There are numerous ways a quarterback can demonstrate leadership. The three great quarterbacks we singled out—Van Brocklin, Unitas, and Montana—all had different styles of commanding others. To say that one method is superior to another would not be fair or accurate. There are many approaches to leading, as can be seen in the careers of greats such as Bart Starr, Warren Moon, Brett Favre, Dan Fouts, Joe Namath, Joe Kapp, Roger Staubach, Terry Bradshaw, Steve Young, Fran Tarkenton, and Dan Marino. In their own way, these quarterbacks were all strong and successful leaders. The common denominator is that their method of leadership worked and worked well.

Success in leadership also depends on a quarterback knowing and understanding his strengths and weaknesses as they relate to his place on the team. To make correct decisions, the quarterback first has to be completely honest with himself. Football games and off-the-field responsibilities require him to use good judgment. The quarterback should ask himself these questions:

- Is this decision mine to make?
- Will my decision be accepted or rejected?
- Will others see this decision as good for the team?
- Am I asking others to do something I myself would not do?
- Do I present my instructions with encouragement and purposefulness?

If the quarterback can ask himself these questions and answer them positively and if he receives positive feedback from others, the indications are excellent that he is on target as a leader.

Handling Challenges

Some quarterbacks are better equipped than others to handle the mental challenges that will confront them. Can the quarterback deal with the pressure, make decisions, manage the clock, anticipate, and do the right things at the right time? Is he capable of making things happen? Does he understand the design of each play, and does he know how to evaluate the performance of others and clarify defensive alignments? Most importantly, does he have the willingness to stand in, regardless of the circumstances, and execute the play? These are critical questions that must be answered to determine the potential of the person playing quarterback. The most anyone should expect is quality execution of the mental and physical tasks that the quarterback must master.

The quarterback will be only as good as his assets allow him to be. Every time a quarterback is asked to do something he is not capable of, it's likely to be a losing effort. However, realize that success lurks around the corner; most aspects of quarterback play can be improved on. With time and effort, the quarterback can improve his skills.

Every Quarterback Needs a Winning Philosophy

No one gets into a fight planning to lose. The reason you play games and keep score is to win. Only noncompetitors don't think winning is what it is all about. Every endeavor in our lives is driven by or based on our desire to succeed and meet our objectives. Winning is the reward for the preparation and hard work that go into getting ready for a contest. The desire to win is that innate quality that demands excellence in all of us. Rules and guidelines are established to give all participants a level playing field, but after that it boils down to the will to win. The goal of winning is an all-the-time, everyday thing. It consumes the tasks we undertake and drives us toward excellence.

Football is regulated by fair play but, at the same time, demands an intense winning attitude from the participants, especially the quarterback. Results often are determined by seconds or inches. The foundation of winning a game is based on judgment decisions, competing under pressure, and a multitude of ongoing disciplines.

What separates football from every other sport is its complexity and tremendous physical and mental abuse. High school and college football teams play far fewer contests than basketball or baseball teams. Therefore, each game involves mucho hours of preparation, multiplying the degree of impact each game has. Winning is what is left when the gun sounds and play is over. It is what motivates us to reach for the final pinnacle, doing everything possible for the reward of winning. We call it "the American way." Nearly every event in our glorious history was tied to the motivation of winning. Our society is tied to competition, and as World War II General George Patton said, "Americans appreciate a winner but won't tolerate a loser." Quarterbacks have to have or at least have to develop a winning outlook, or a team will have little chance for success.

Please do not misunderstand the philosophy of winning. There is much to learn whether you win or lose. Understand, however, that the goal is to win. All anyone can expect out of another is the best that person has to offer, which is an all-out effort. The problem is many don't give it their best shot because they don't really know how good they are or could be. Some accept defeat far too easily.

▪ A successful quarterback can perform under pressure and displays a fierce winning attitude.

Players often do not know what a total commitment means, that only with solid effort does anyone win. Only by an extended all-out consistent performance can you overcome obstacles. I have heard it said you can't win without the horses. The truth is that a team is stuck with the horses it has and where it finishes in the race depends on what it does with those horses. How many games are lost because the team is willing to accept losses? It's best not to think negatively on what a team doesn't have but rather have confidence that the job can be done one way or another with those who are available.

A versatile, intelligent quarterback can be the compensating factor for any team without enough horses. A big part of helping a team grow toward winning is accepting how things are and making the most out of every opportunity. It's a matter of never being satisfied or content and continuously striving to make the situation better. When this is done, it's likely that winning and success will follow. More times than not, refusing to accept situations as they are leads to change. No player in the game today can effect and bring about change like the quarterback.

Modern Quarterbacks

Few will doubt that the modern quarterback has more tools at his disposal than yesterday's signal caller. Sophisticated pads, a textured football with an improved shape, and use of videotape, among other things, make quarterbacking more dynamic. Some question, however, the type of persons who play the position today, saying they don't care enough or do enough to be great quarterbacks. To be a quarterback demands a heavy price, and many players are unwilling to spend the time that the position requires. Most quarterbacks sacrifice endlessly, however, to be the key player for their team.

A committed quarterback is visible and obvious to those evaluating. All you have to do is attend a game and witness firsthand the results of the hours a particular quarterback put in so that he could perform successfully. A field general committed to excellence is the heart of any team and is a must to develop or maintain a competitive program. Henry Ford said it best: "Whether you think you can or you think you can't, you're right."

The quarterback is almost always alone with his many responsibilities. Quarterbacks more than anyone else must embrace their responsibilities and accept the challenge as part of the nature of being a signal caller. They have a huge duty, and no one claims the task is easy.

The position of quarterback in this day and age simply is not for everybody. The job is extremely demanding and almost limitless in scope. These days, no football player is held more accountable for his actions, or his team's actions, than the quarterback. Not one athlete is expected to influence winning more than the quarterback. He is one of a kind, leading his team in a physical sport that demands his best every time he lines up behind the center. The average fan seems to expect a picture-perfect effort each and every play and in all games. The coach often calls the young man who accepts this position his dominant player. Fans and players look to the quarterback to bring about winning. Fans also expect the quarterback to make the game exciting and entertaining. So it is in the life of the modern-day signal caller.

Character Counts

The saying "Good guys finish first" provides the theme and description for the ideal quarterback with respect to being an example. A major factor in winning is a player's devotion to improvement. Whom a player looks up to and respects often affects that person's outlook and philosophy.

Caring about others helps us become better people, as we develop strong bonds. In the family and the community, at church, and in school, caring about others is promoted. Each of these enviroments can have a positive influence on a quarterback, and these relationships make any quarterback a more effective player. A well-rounded person is able to influence those around him in different ways, which in turn improves the mood of the team. Appropriate associations strengthen the quarterback's image as a role model to his peers, both on and off the field. The quarterback learns a little more about being a total person. His example tends to spill over onto the team, often with positive results. Francis Bacon once said, "If a man will begin with certainties, he shall end in doubt; but if he will be content to begin with doubts, he shall end in certainties." Doubts are unknown and can be eliminated when a quarterback finds out just what life, as well as football, is all about.

Mental Preparation Is Critical

Regardless of the amount of talent he has or coaching he receives, a quarterback's passport to success is always tied to hard work. When there is blood, sweat, and tears, you have a winning formula. Although this statement may not be totally valid, there is no substitute for hard work. There are no quick fixes or easy paths to results.

Every quarterback, regardless of the environment, performs according to his preparation. When committed, the quarterback almost always will be the guy who makes the fewest mistakes and the one seen as the disciplined athlete, the prepared player. A quarterback who moves the team is well drilled and has developed real insight into the job at hand. The signal caller who creates the big play developed poise and confidence long before the game. It is no accident that some quarterbacks win more games than others. Quarterbacks improve when they are fine-tuned and well equipped. Conversely, some regress because they are not deeply involved; they soon become casualties of the position.

Attitude, Motivation, and Commitment to the System

If we were to design a mental formula for quarterbacking, the first ingredient would be appropriate attitude, which reflects the quarterback's outlook. The next ingredient is motivation and a constant dedication to the content of his job description. Third is to compete within and be totally loyal to the philosophy and system of play. When the quarterback displays continuous self-discipline, then team discipline is likely to follow.

All of these elements encompass the mental part of the game that a quarterback must deal with every day. How he manages the mental game will determine his success, as well as that of his teammates, in any given contest or season.

Vince Lombardi and others have said that winning is most of all an attitude. A winning quarterback is one who won't let others down. This athlete gives 100 percent all of the time regardless of circumstances. Consistent productive performance by any team reflects the quarterback's mental qualities and state of mind.

Often a coach's evaluation of a quarterback is limited to dealing with his physical ability. Physical ability sometimes makes first downs, but it doesn't always win the game. The old adage "Give me a winning attitude and I will win" has much merit. Many games are won as a result of timely decision making, execution, poise, and preparation rather than simply dominating athletic ability.

A common misconception is that we are who we are and nothing can change that. Rather, it should be stated that we are what we want to be and almost everything, to a point, can change. Playing quarterback is difficult, but it is easier when there is a complete understanding of the role. This is why it's so important that the quarterback assumes the heavy burden of committing to being as good as he can possibly be.

Good Decisions, Appropriate Action

Good things happen if the when-and-what decisions are correctly made by the quarterback. When to do what makes all the difference in the world. A quarterback has everything to do with progress if he is right with his decisions. What to do and when to do it mean correct timing and often are as important as technique or execution in football. The quarterback creates successful timing. When to use a long count or go on first sound, when to use an audible to change a play, and whom to throw to are just some of the decisions a field general must decide regularly.

In the off-season, workout emphases are paramount to development. What is said and done to prepare during a game week will affect game results. Allotting time to work on last week's mistakes, perfecting a specific skill, or studying the game plan can and does make an enormous difference in a quarterback's and his team's readiness to compete at their best.

Making the Call

One of the best examples of wise, perceptive quarterback play occurred in our 1995 National Championship game against Marshall University.

It was fourth down with 12 yards to go and less than one minute left in the game. Dave Dickenson, our extremely talented quarterback, recognized that the Marshall's defensive coverage was going to overwhelm the pass play that was called in the huddle. On the line of scrimmage, Dave checked to another play. Dave got away from a combination pattern to an individual route to take advantage of Marshall's deployment of secondary personnel.

The play succeeded. We obtained a first down, which allowed the drive to continue. The end result was we overcame Marshall's 20 to 19 lead and won the game. Dave's decision reflected ingenuity, football savvy, and poise. These assets are as important as any physical attribute a field general can feature. In our case, Dave's creativity brought the University of Montana its first ever national championship.

Mannerisms

Through his expressions, body actions, and general mannerisms, a quarterback can emphasize whatever he wants to get across to his teammates. Using his arms, head, upper body, and fingers, he can stress almost any area he desires. His voice, too, when used right, can carry a message, adding meaning for those tuned in. Facial expressions usually assist in getting the information across to the listener quickly and clearly.

Body movement, expression, and voice pitch provide added meaning to a quarterback's communication skills. When a quarterback learns how, when, and where to incorporate body language, he becomes more effective at playing his position. All of these expressive actions can be worked on and changed for the better.

Build Around Physical Assets

The real insightfulness of quarterbacking is allowing the quarterback to do what he can do best within the system of play. The flip side of this is not to ask him to do something that he is unable to do. This truly is the best way to make the quarterback effective and the team successful.

▪ Dan Fouts was a standout quarterback at the University of Oregon. His precision, toughness, and quickness led him to a successful NFL career.

It should be apparent that there needs to be continual and careful analysis of the strengths and weaknesses of a quarterback's skills. When the results of this analysis are applied, the offensive attack can absorb the talent and feature it. Winning always reflects appropriate use of the personnel at hand, particularly the field general.

There are countless examples of teams who used the talents of their quarterback to the fullest and won big. The great professional football organization of the '60s was the Green Bay Packers. That team used play action passes off of their powerful running game to score many touchdowns. Bart Starr, the quarterback of that team, was a master at ball handling. A team that is run oriented also can win games with the pass by using this tactic.

Perhaps the best example of using the quarterback's skills correctly and molding an offense around what he could do was demonstrated by the San Diego Chargers of the late '70s and early '80s. Dan Fouts, the quarterback for those teams, was as good as anyone has ever been at throwing the ball with precision. He was mentally tough, perceptive, and could get rid of the ball quickly. These assets were built into San Diego's offense and led to numerous NFL records being shattered. That obviously equated to many games being won.

The mobility of Steve Young propelled the San Francisco 49ers to division titles and a Super Bowl victory in the '90s. This extremely gifted athlete literally picked defenses apart with his feet. He gave himself time to throw by being mobile in and out of the pocket, which in turn limited the defensive linemen's ability to zero in on him. Bill Walsh and George Seifert, 49er coaches of that time, perfected the popular West Coast offense around Young's quick feet and arm, which truly paid off big.

In the college and high school ranks, many quarterbacks are chosen to play because their physical abilities fit the needs of the system. Whether a quarterback is selected for his ability to play within a specific offense or a coach tailors an offense to what a particular athlete can do best doesn't matter. What counts is that the offense and the quarterback are compatible. Successful strategy always is to combine assets with a designed system of play.

Think of the quarterback–offense relationship in terms of a glove and hand. To best serve the hand, the glove must fit correctly. A hand cannot function properly unless the glove is suitable. When a quarterback has inadequate skills to perform in a given offense, he is likely to be unproductive. More times than not, the team also is ineffective. There is nothing more important to an offense than a positive mesh between the quarterback and the offensive system. If the offense doesn't comply with the quarterback's skills or his abilities don't fit within the offense, then it will show in the number of losses.

Physical Characteristics

As with Bart Starr, Dan Fouts, and Steve Young, quarterbacks can be great if they master at least one physical skill—ball handling, quick release or precision, or mobility. Using these talents appropriately can make an average team into a good team. It's a matter of identifying adaption.

Each quarterback's unique physical makeup may determine which skill he emphasizes. His God-given physical dimensions—his weight, height, and other more subtle traits—carry unique advantages and disadvantages. Often the less obvious characteristics are the most important.

Long arms often convert to potential throwing distance, but they often mean slower delivery. Shorter arms frequently convert to quicker mechanics. A thicker chest and longer torso also are factors.

Excellent vision, both depth perception and peripheral, can be a tremendous asset for a quarterback. The more he sees and can adjust his vision, the better a quarterback he can be. Being able to see effectively at night and having equally good vision in both eyes can make a difference in how he plays the position.

Leg length is a factor in quarterback performance. Much like arms, leg length correlates to quicker or slower movement. Long legs are not advantageous unless the quarterback heads an offense that requires straightaway speed because most long-legged quarterbacks are long striders. Shorter legs often mean a quicker-moving quarterback. For a quarterback, quickness is more important than speed in most offensive attacks. By quickness, I mean the ability to react or move swiftly for a short time in a given direction. Speed can be defined as rapid movement in a straight line.

A final ingredient is physical strength. A quarterback who has a strong lower and upper body gains many advantages over the guy who lacks these assets. Lower-body strength is a big factor in running with the football but also in taking on rushers when passing. Solid upper-body strength aids throwing and absorbing the force of an oncoming tackler.

More than anything else, physical durability has become critical to the position of quarterback. One only has to check the starting lineups of the high school, college, or professional ranks to find quarterbacks who cannot play because of injury. Football is a physical game, and it takes a physical person to play quarterback. His height, weight, body makeup, flexibility, speed, quickness, and overall body strength relate to how well he will play the position.

About Hall of Famers

Greatness normally presents itself at the end of a long journey. How can a quarterback get better at playing his position during his journey? Contrary to what many people think, great quarterbacks are not always born; often, they are made. They do what they can do and become what they can become. It is important to know that there has never been an outstanding quarterback who has not worked hard at mastering the position—not Johnny Unitas, Joe Montana, John Elway, Dan Fouts, Dan Marino, Bobby Layne, Otto Graham, or the many others who could be mentioned. They all put their time in and paid their dues. Each and every one of them got better because of two critical components: attitude and effort. They developed good work habits; then those habits continued to develop them. A signal caller will usually get as long as he is willing to give.

You can bet these supertalents were told at some point one or more of the following things:

- You are not heavy enough.
- You are too slow.
- You don't have enough arm.
- You are not as tall as you need to be.
- You lack foot speed.
- Your delivery is too slow.
- You need experience.
- You don't have the poise or self-discipline to be successful.
- You lack confidence or self-image.

These Hall of Famers became the best because they didn't listen to their critics. They believed in themselves and set out on a mission to prove disbelievers wrong. What can be learned from this? Some signal callers are more gifted in one area than others, but it is what lies in the mind and heart that influences performance the most. Physical traits do play a major part but are simply the foundation. To be the best, it helps to be gifted, but some of the greatest were not. Obviously not every quarterback is destined for the Hall of Fame, but all can improve by adopting a Hall of Fame attitude.

CHAPTER 2

STANCE-TO-SNAP FUNDAMENTALS

The right stance plus a good exchange likely result in a well-executed play. Simple as it sounds, every play has a beginning and an end. The appropriate start gives the play a chance for a productive finish. While speaking on the importance of quarterback stance and exchange, Norv Turner, former head coach of the Washington Redskins, said it best: "You can't make a big play without proper handling of the football."

The quarterback is always the critical player when it comes to doing the right thing with the football. His fundamentals are imperative to all his teammates' involvement and their effectiveness within the system. Stance-to-snap fundamentals appear to be simple, which they are, but their importance cannot be overstated. Appropriate technique from the quarterback does not guarantee perfect exchanges, but correct execution in putting the ball into play will definitely lower the fumble rate.

Have you ever seen a signal caller approach the line of scrimmage and align behind a guard instead of the center? It's the epitome of embarrassment and is not the right thing to do when preparing to start a play. It's humorous, and there is a reason it happens. From the time the quarterback leaves the huddle until he lines up behind the center, he has a ton of preparation to do for the upcoming play. The information he gathers as he approaches the line assists him in making the best out of the situation at hand.

At this point, the quarterback can't allow his heart to bypass his brain. The most pertinent facts he gathers include identifying the number of defensive linemen, noting the alignment of the defense, counting the number of linebackers, evaluating the secondary, and identifying the potential coverage. In short, he is surveying the opposition's game plan strategy and adjustments.

During the walkup, the quarterback determines whether the play is likely to be successful. If there is to be an automatic call or change of play, the time between huddle and snap is when the decision often is made. Alignment and formation also are checked and changed if necessary.

The Stance

The quarterback's stance is important for many reasons. In fact, correct play execution depends on the appropriateness of his stance. Notice the word "appropriateness" here. There are no absolutes with respect to stance; it's customized to the offense used and the quarterback's body type.

The nature of the quarterback's stance too often is taken for granted. Proper stance technique can make the exchange from center routine; bad stance technique can create a fumble. The handoff or push back to throw or pitch is affected by the quarterback's stance. Quarterbacks vary as to body build and arm length, which affect both stance and exchange. How much a quarterback bends his knees and how far from the center he lines up have to do with his body type.

Another element that influences stance is the type of offense being run. Some offenses require specific foot placement to enable the quarterback to best function. With these factors in mind, let's examine two types of stances, run oriented and pass oriented.

Run-Oriented Stance

Generally speaking, a run-oriented offensive attack requires the quarterback to be in a balanced or semibalanced stance (figure 2.1). The balanced toe-to-toe stance allows a quarterback to move to his left or right equally well. (Some run-oriented offenses and most pass offenses require the quarterback to switch to a staggered stance, which permits a good push back and quick separation from the line of scrimmage.)

Figure 2.1

 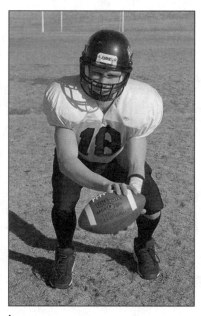

a   b

Run-dominated offense requires (*a*) a balanced or (*b*) semibalanced stance.

Distance from the football or the center's buttocks also may be affected by the style of the offense. There should be adequate ride for the quarterback as the center moves with the snap. This normally is about 12 inches but can be less or more depending on whether the quarterback primarily moves down the line of scrimmage or away from it to execute the offense. While the quarterback is in position to receive the football, his elbows are pointed slightly outward and down. Without moving his feet, the quarterback follows the buttocks of the center while securing the football.

The quarterback's shoulders should be rounded inward and his back relatively straight. His head is up and his buttocks are down, forcing some bend in the knees. The ideal balanced stance places the quarterback much closer to the center, permitting him to operate out of a lower profile. The width of his feet should not exceed the width of his shoulders. The feet are slightly staggered and toed in, with weight equally distributed on the balls of the feet.

Pass-Oriented Stance

Staggering the feet in the stance means left foot back for a right-handed quarterback and right foot back for a left-handed quarterback. The distance between the feet should be narrower than that of a balanced stance but not less than the width of the quarterback's hips (figure 2.2). A toe-to-heel or instep relationship is about right. Weight should be about 60 percent on the foot farthest away from the football.

It is not necessary for the quarterback to lower himself as much as he would if he were using a balanced stance. There must be, however, enough knee bend to allow the receiving hand, the upper one, to be flat under the center's buttocks. Because the staggered stance allows the quarterback to pull away from the line of scrimmage, and the center does not fire straight upfield as often in passing plays, the quarterback can have less knee bend. He should keep his weight farther back.

Figure 2.2

Pass-dominated offense requires a staggered stance.

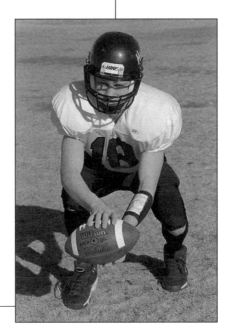

Cadence and Calling Plays

Like stance, cadence goes along with the nature of offense. Some types of cadence are more beneficial to a given offense. For example, the best choice for a zone-blocking, run-oriented attack might be a quick rhythm count. More sophisticated offenses may feature changing plays at the line of scrimmage or drop-back passing and often use a nonrhythm cadence. Some offenses choose a blend of both rhythm and nonrhythm cadences.

Some teams tie together the play called and the count. In other words, the snap goes with the play. Other teams go on first sound and occasionally use a long count for a change-up.

These are some things to consider when adopting a cadence:

- Is it simple enough for all to master without mishap?
- Does the cadence help the play of the offense?
- Is the cadence flexible? Does it allow for change?

The most common words used in cadence are "hut" and "go":

- For a rhythm cadence: "hut-hut-hut" or "go-go-go"
- For a nonrhythm cadence: "hut-huthut-hut" or "go-gogo-go"

It's best to preface the cadence with a word or two such as "ready" or "set" or both. These precadence words prepare players for the cadence to follow. Precadence words also give the offense the option of starting the play on one of these words, which is a good way to hold the defensive rush in check.

The quarterback's voice projection can also add to the effectiveness of the cadence. Former Miami Dolphins quarterback Dan Marino and Green Bay's quarterback Brett Favre mastered the art of drawing the opposition offside with their voice projection. When a quarterback barks out certain words with more volume and a defense is trying to anticipate the count, the defense often will jump offside. A method frequently used is for the quarterback to slow down his count and then come out strong with a given word. Another way to execute voice projection is to stay with the count being used, and on the "hut" or "go" as the get-off sound, project deep and loud on that word.

Automatics—changing the play at the line of scrimmage—should be placed in an offense by building the automatic call into the cadence. The most common labeling of automatics in football today is colors and numbers, call number or play in cadence, and the use of an opposite word to flip the same play to the other side of the formation (see table 2.1).

A color or number auto method in the cadence would go like this: "Red, 32" or "blue, 32." A predetermined live color is used as an indicator to change a called play. If red is the live color, the play is changed to 32. If blue or any other color is called, the play chosen in the huddle is run, because blue is a dead color. The quarterback would say, "set," the color (live or dead), the play number, and "hut."

The call number or play method involves calling a live or dead number instead of a color. After the live number is called, the play is changed to the number called after the live number. If a dead number is used, the play number that follows is a dummy (for example,

Table 2.1   Approaches to Automatic Calls

Method	If play is changing . . .		If play is staying the same . . .	
	Cadence	Result	Cadence	Result
Live and dead colors	QB calls predetermined live color, then the number of the play (e.g., "red, 32")	Play switches from the play called in the huddle to play 32	QB calls any other color (the dead color), then a play number (e.g., "blue, 32")	Play called in the huddle is run
Call number	QB calls predetermined live number, then the number of the play (e.g., "10, 28")	Play switches from the play called in the huddle to play 28	QB calls any other number (the dead number), then any play number (e.g., "20, 28")	Play called in the huddle is run
Opposite word	QB calls "opposite" and then the number of the play (e.g., "opposite, 28")	Play called in the huddle switches direction to the other side of the field	QB does not say "opposite" during his cadence	Play called in the huddle is run to the side originally planned

"set, 10, 28, hut"). If 10 is the live number, 28 becomes the play. If 10 is not the live number, the play to be run is the one determined in the huddle and 28 is just a smoke screen.

A third approach to building autos in the cadence is to use the word "opposite." When opposite is called, the play is mirrored to the opposite side of the line of scrimmage. The same play is run to the side opposite the one chosen in the huddle.

All three methods of automatic calling are good and relatively simple. The auto part of the cadence should be called twice, or the quarterback should pause for at least one second after the auto and before the starting count begins. This allows the offense to digest the change of play.

When calling the cadence, the quarterback should project his voice by moving his head from left to right during the count. Whatever procedure he uses must be consistent in every play so that his teammates can anticipate the procedure and any possible changes that may occur. This includes words used, rhythm, pauses, and the length of the cadence itself.

Receiving the Snap

There are three aspects of receiving a snap from the center. Each component to a degree blends with the others. These elements are positioning the hands, securing the ball, and riding the center.

Hand position refers to the placement of the receiving hand and securing hand. The receiving hand is the quarterback's throwing hand and serves as a target for the center-to-quarterback exchange. The middle finger on the receiving hand needs to apply lifting pressure under the crotch of the center. This hand should be under the center's buttocks to the wrist, with the fingers stretched for width. To ensure that the receiving hand is relatively flat and comfortable in alignment, the quarterback has to bend his knees to assume the correct elevation and position.

The football should strike all the fingers simultaneously. The heel of the securing hand needs to be in contact with the receiving hand, with the thumbs pointing parallel to each other (figure 2.3). The larger the quarterback's hands, the easier it is for him to execute this part of the exchange. When the football comes up from the center, the quarterback should receive the ball with the laces hitting slightly off center to the middle finger of his receiving hand. The ball will make contact with the quarterback's hand at a slight angle

Figure 2.3

The QB's hands should be in contact, with the thumbs parallel.

across the fingers. The position of the football will be almost flat, with a little elevation, and slightly forward to the center's left leg, assuming the center is right handed.

The securing hand (the left hand if the quarterback is right handed) then collapses around the lower part of the ball. The fingers of the securing hand should be pointed down toward the ground. The action of the securing hand not only traps the ball but firmly pushes it up into the receiving hand so that the quarterback can grip the ball. With two hands on the football, the quarterback is now ready to position it in his hands for handing off, pitching, or passing. If the football is not to be handed off or pitched immediately, it should be brought close to his body.

Riding the center is the final and critical part of the exchange. The relationship of the quarterback's feet and arms to the center is what allows for the ride. Basically, the closer the quarterback is to the center, the longer the ride. Because the ride is done exclusively with the arm, the elbow must be bent to provide for arm extension of about 12 inches. The ride constitutes the time the ball is coming up and the point where the quarterback has the ball secured. During the ride, the center takes his first step in his blocking assignment so that this pulling away creates separation between the quarterback and center (figure 2.4). The ride also involves the quarterback staying in contact with the center as he, too, is pulling away from the center. A quarterback should be able to ride by extending his arms out about a foot, so his arms must be bent at the elbows. Not enough arm bend shortens the ride and can increase the chances of a poor exchange. If the quarterback has to step forward to ensure receiving the snap, he will slow down the overall play execution, giving the defense an advantage. The ride guarantees both securing the football and proper footwork for the play selected to begin in a timely fashion.

Figure 2.4

The ride.

As the center snaps the ball, he steps into his blocking assignment, separating himself from the QB.

Exchange Problems

Exchange problems and fumbles are generally the fault of the quarterback. The quarterback needs to alter his stance to the center's buttocks by changing his knee bend when fumbles occur. The depth of the quarterback's hands under the center's buttocks is another major culprit in causing mishaps on exchange. Another common cause for ball-exchange mishaps is when the football does not strike the quarterback's throwing hand correctly as he receives the ball.

Perfecting all stance-to-snap fundamentals can be done by keeping the center and quarterback together for the maximum time allowed during practice. This means when centers are in run-blocking drills, the quarterback should take exchanges. When quarterback–receiver drills are in session, the center needs to be present to provide the exchange. Prepractice or postpractice quarterback–center exchange drills can also be incorporated. The process of stance and exchange, as with everything else in football, can be improved and refined. The more realistic the exchange process, the smoother and more successful the procedure. Making the center block a person or a bag during quarterback–center work is gamelike and ideal.

A last consideration in perfecting this process is using still photos. Pictures of the hand position, ball, angles, and hit point can show problems that need adjustment. This visual account can help the quarterback better understand the exchange.

CHAPTER 3

HANDOFFS, FAKES, AND PITCHES

Execution is everything if a team is to have a running attack that moves the ball. What the quarterback does and how he does it are like gasoline to a car—he makes the play go. A quarterback with proper position, footwork, hand–eye coordination, and timing is the catalyst for each play an offense runs. The better he is at executing the finer elements within the basic fundamentals of quarterback play, the more effective the running attack will be. Because all physical skills can be improved, it comes down to committing time and energy to perfect the various components involved in the wide range of skills called quarterback fundamentals.

Great athletes sometimes can ignore one fundamental or another. For most signal callers, however, poor basics spell disaster. A superior quarterback can be even more accomplished if his fundamentals are sound. Running game execution for a quarterback is precise on every play, and every movement depends on his preciseness.

The field general's handling of the football means everything to a team's running attack. The where, when, and how of each ball-handling situation are totally in the hands of the quarterback. He determines how each play will begin and provides the subtle judgment that goes with each running play to make it work. In the final analysis, a quarterback hands off the football or pitches it 30 to 50 times a game on average. Therefore, the quarterback's worth in the running game can't be stressed enough. When a team features a conventional running attack, the quarterback's input should not be underestimated. He has a lot to do with whatever success the running game produces. All running plays depend on the field general's skill and consistency. Nonbelievers should ask any running back the importance of properly receiving the football from the quarterback. An even greater confirmation would come from a coach if he were asked about the effect that turnovers have on a game.

There is a correct way to handle a football. Unfortunately, there is an incorrect way. Proper ball handling can provide a winning edge. Field generals differ widely in their physical and mental capabilities, but correct play-starting fundamentals are a requirement for all quarterbacks. Without precision ball handling, handoffs, fakes, and pitches are left to chance.

Winning With Quarterback Execution

You've heard it said that if it doesn't work, change it. Not so when dealing with the quarterback's football basics. The quarterback's actions are the foundation for all running game execution and must be constant. Booker T. Washington once said, "Excellence is doing a common thing in an uncommon way." Execution is fundamental, but good execution adds flare to the play.

Quarterback fundamentals, particularly in any running package, take on several basic components. These factors are footwork, weight distribution, ball location, head and eye position, knee bend, and body angle. Each of these elements exists to reciprocate to the others in some manner. Mechanics used in the running game often complement the movements used in passing.

A quarterback's feet, which are his most important asset, provide him with his best chance to succeed at executing running game fundamentals. Correct foot position at the exchange point ensures proper mesh with the ball carrier. There are, however, some other common traits that are basic to all forms of quarterback movement. These characteristics are critical for quality ball handling and will be stressed in the following pages as each signal caller fundamental is presented in this chapter.

Regardless of the fundamental being used, a quarterback has to maintain a football position (knees bent, buttocks down, back straight; see figure 3.1) to execute any of his skills in a running attack. This position gives the quarterback a good solid base for balance and maneuverability. Faking and all ball handling begin during and from this body alignment.

Figure 3.1

The football position provides a secure base for the QB to execute running plays.

From a solid football position, a quarterback is better able to demonstrate good foot spacing. Location of the quarterback's feet is essential at the exchange point, as there needs to be reasonable clearance between the field general and prospective ball carrier to enable the ball carrier to function correctly. Ideally the quarterback's foot and hand (lead or trail) on the same side should work together at the handoff point, although this cannot always be done. The distance between the quarterback's feet and the ball carrier at the exchange point should be at least 12 inches to allow for proper mesh, faking, and appropriate handoffs.

Handoffs

All exchanges to a ball carrier should be made with two hands giving way to one. For example, a right-handed quarterback takes the exchange from the center (figure 3.2a), with his right hand slightly turned upward on the football, while the left hand is placed to the side and turned under at about a 45-degree angle. After securing the ball with his left hand for grip, the quarterback moves to the handoff location with the football in both hands (figure 3.2b), carrying it as close to his body as possible until he begins to reach to the ball carrier to exchange the ball. The ball is rotated to a two-handed balanced grip (figure 3.2c) while being carried. Both sides of the football must be held firmly with both hands at about the middle of the ball.

Figure 3.2

The handoff.

(*a*) The QB takes the exchange from the center.

(*b*) He carries the ball in both hands as he moves to the handoff point.

(*c*) Holding the ball in a two-handed balanced grip, the QB reaches with the ball toward the RB.

(*d*) The QB's hand nearest the RB comes off the ball as the QB hands off to the RB.

When the quarterback reaches to put the ball on the belly button of the running back, he rotates the hand closest to the ball carrier downward. The hand nearest the ball carrier comes off the ball as rotation of the hand begins (figure 3.2d). The hand nearest the line of scrimmage slides back toward the quarterback as he pulls it away from the exchange point or first arm contact with the ball carrier.

This technique minimizes exchange problems and fumbles by keeping the hand nearest the ball carrier from getting between the ball and the running back. The quarterback should always make handoffs without overextending his reach, which is when the quarterback's weight is totally on the toes of his lead foot.

Ball Security

The quarterback must always keep his feet under him. During the exchange, there is the danger of the quarterback getting overextended with his reach, particularly when executing the reverse pivot or backpedal from the line of scrimmage. Shorter steps and a wider base are good precautionary tactics to prevent this from happening. Keeping knees bent also aids balance and stability as the quarterback executes this basic fundamental in handing the ball off or faking.

The abdomen and hips can act as a third hand to keep the football secured during quarterback action on run plays. Anytime the ball is carried away from the body, the chance of fumbling increases. Correct grip (two hands on the ball) is a solid fundamental tip for protecting the football during the entire exchange process (figure 3.3).

The arms and hands permit reach, help hide the football, and protect it from mishaps. Hands can cover the point of the football for security reasons or grip the laces for tossing, pitching, or passing. The quarterback should carry the ball with both hands when possible and shift the football to the arm and hand away from the opponent. The arm should be used to cover the football when the quarterback himself is carrying the football in traffic. The quarterback should keep his shoulders level and low when running with the ball, as might be the case in option, sprint-out, or bootleg plays, or when taking on a tackler.

Figure 3.3

Correct two-handed grip.

Deception in Run Fakes

A quarterback's eyes and/or head can go a long way to freeze or misdirect the opposition. Just because the ball carrier goes one direction doesn't mean the quarterback has to be a spectator and watch. He can and should instead look elsewhere, attempting to influence the other team. Following a fake handoff with his eyes and head can also neutralize opponent pursuit angles or delay his chase. This procedure is particularly effective on plays such as boot or misdirection actions. Using the body as a shield, the football can be hidden on most plays until the exchange occurs.

Footwork

Quarterback maneuvering skills can be classified as front out, reverse pivot, sprint drop, and backpedal. Use of any or all of these actions depends on the type of offense employed. A quarterback should be able to execute these actions with exact precision. There are other quarterback fundamentals less frequently used, but these four form the foundation for quarterback movement.

▪ Front out. The quarterback steps with his lead foot in the direction he wants to go. He can be releasing at an angle or straight down the line. Fronting out is used in an option attack, when handing the ball off on or about the line of scrimmage. It may involve a short or long first step, once again depending on the play called. If the lead step is short, the trail foot will cross over. If the open step is long, the trail step should not be a crossover. The front-out technique is the fastest way to get to a given point (figure 3.4).

Figure 3.4

Front out.

(*a*) The QB first steps with his lead foot in the direction he wants to go.

(*b*) He then steps with his trail foot.

- Reverse pivot (figure 3.5). One foot will cross over the stationary foot. The stationary foot serves as the push step in the pivot move. The crossover foot establishes the appropriate angle and distance. A reverse-pivot motion almost always hides the football well because on his first step the quarterback has his back to the line of scrimmage. The quarterback spins away from his initial body movement.

Figure 3.5

Reverse pivot.

(*a*) The QB crosses one foot over the other, his back to the line of scrimmage.

(*b*) The QB then turns his body away from his initial movement.

▪ Sprint drop. The sprint drop allows the quarterback to go straight back from the center to the running back. This action features a first-step pull away from center, straight back move (figure 3.6). Draw, trap, or delayed handoffs often incorporate this technique. The move looks much like the three-, five-, and seven-step drops used in the passing game, and the footwork is the same. The first leg movement is always a reach, or extended step, followed by a shorter crossover.

Figure 3.6

Sprint drop.

(*a*) The QB stands behind the center.

(b) The QB steps straight back away from the center.

(c) Then he uses a shorter crossover step.

- Backpedal. The quarterback begins by taking a large drop step with the foot nearest the center (figure 3.7). The second step with the other foot is shorter, keeping the body square to the line of scrimmage. The third step is like the first, a larger step straight back, while the fourth step follows with the other foot, and so on. Steps are naturally shorter because striding backward is restricted in ways that don't have to be dealt with when moving forward. The back out, or backpedal technique, is often used in the running game when a draw, fake draw, inside handoff, or counter-type play is run. Backpedaling is commonly used with a right-handed quarterback when the throw is to the left.

Figure 3.7

Backpedal.

(*a*) The QB stands behind the center.

(*b*) He takes a long drop step with the foot nearest the center.

(*c*) Then he takes a shorter step, keeping his body square to the LOS.

Carrying the Football

There are a number of ways to hold the ball, but there is only one right way. The correct way is to place one tip of the ball in the armpit, covering the other point with the fingers on the hand of that arm (figure 3.8). The position between the biceps and breast offers leverage on the ball. Carrying the football in this manner is not only safe but natural. This is not to say a football can't be carried away from the body or in the hands, but around the opposition these methods are dangerous. When carrying the ball into heavy traffic, the nonholding hand should cover the ball to ensure ball protection.

Figure 3.8

When carrying the ball into traffic, the QB should use his other hand to cover the ball and protect it.

Bootleg

One of the least used yet most effective ways to cause havoc for a defense is to show running back flow in a given direction while the quarterback hides the ball after the fake and goes another way (figure 3.9). This type of fake has been used in football ever since the time helmets could be folded up and carried in a pocket. This faking action is effective and popular for many reasons.

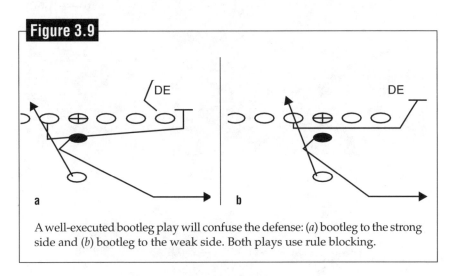

Figure 3.9

a

b

A well-executed bootleg play will confuse the defense: (*a*) bootleg to the strong side and (*b*) bootleg to the weak side. Both plays use rule blocking.

The quarterback gives a long arm-extended fake after taking the proper angle to the mesh point, then brings the football into his body (figure 3.10). The quarterback holds the ball in his abdominal area, then slides it to his back-side hip as he comes off the exchange fake. To help create the illusion that the running back has the football, the quarterback must follow the back's path with his eyes. By turning the shoulder farthest from the line of scrimmage away from the direction of the ball carrier and rotating his head away from the direction he is moving, the quarterback can sell the fake to the defense. The fake should be held until the quarterback's path extends beyond the tight end position.

Figure 3.10

The bootleg play.

(*a*) The QB must sell the fake handoff to the RB.

(*b*) The QB hides the ball after the fake but follows the RB with his eyes.

Zone and rotating-to-flow coverage defenses (discussed in chapter 9) are almost always caught going the wrong direction because of the quarterback's action. Overactive linebackers tend to scrape and pursue away from the ball, as the action of play influences their path. A good bootleg maneuver off an often-used play becomes big for a run offense. Bootleg plays do not have to be run only, because pass plays can be effective using the same fundamental technique. These are the keys to a successful bootleg play:

- Quarterback and running back execute a convincing fake at the exchange point.
- Running back carries out his fake.
- Quarterback hides the ball from the defense.
- Quarterback uses his head, eyes, and shoulder rotation to follow the movement of the running back.
- Quarterback takes correct angle to rush point and three to five steps beyond.

Pitching the Football

Pitching the ball involves flipping the football with a live spinning action that duplicates the rotation of a forward pass. The pitch is relatively fast with a spiraling movement. The ball is pitched underhand using a front-out or reverse-pivot move by the quarterback. The laces provide grip and leverage on the football and are used to accelerate the twisting of the ball. This action not only gets the ball to the target faster but propels it more accurately.

Pitching the football is most successfully used when the ball needs to travel a distance greater than six yards (for example, when a back flares from an alignment behind or outside of his offensive tackle). Pitches can also be used when a reverse-pivot quarterback technique is used on a pitch play.

If the quarterback is right handed, his right hand is the pitch hand, and the left hand secures and guides the ball until it comes off the hand naturally. The quarterback needs to step directly at the running back's receiving point when he pitches (figure 3.11). Pitches always have to lead the potential ball carrier by one to two yards, about waist high.

Figure 3.11

The pitch.

(*a*) The QB steps directly toward the RB's receiving point.

(*b*) The pitch needs to lead the ball carrier by one to two yards and be thrown about waist high.

The velocity of the ball should not be too fast but not soft, making the pitch easy to catch. Recommended speed for the football during its flight is three-fourths of the quarterback's maximum top effort.

Tossing the Football

For a toss, the football is flipped with two hands in a dead or tumbling manner. The quarterback grips the middle of the ball. One form of the toss is to push the ball from about chest high, with the quarterback in a football position. Another common form is to flip it underhanded with two hands (figure 3.12).

These techniques are used when running the option or tossing to a running back on a sweep action–type play. No doubt there are many advantages to using the toss over the pitch method, but being easier to catch leads the list. There is a place for both of these forms of lateral passes.

Figure 3.12

To toss the football, the QB can use two hands to toss the ball underhanded to the ball carrier.

Waggle Action

In the waggle action, the quarterback starts in one direction and finishes in another (figure 3.13). Waggle action generally means misdirection, so the quarterback must hide the ball by staying relatively low during the entire process.

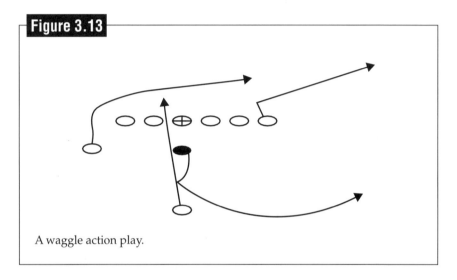

Figure 3.13

A waggle action play.

This movement is often used on double dives or crossing-back plays. However, it can also be incorporated into fake inside– and give outside–type plays. Waggle action also is frequently used in a team's passing game by faking a run and waggling to one side or the other. The technique can be executed from the open/front-out or reverse-pivot approach. The most common use of waggle movement is to fake the run in a given direction and give the ball off, with another back going in another direction (figure 3.14). Unlike bootleg, the quarterback does not generally flow beyond the alignment of his offensive tackle.

Figure 3.14

The waggle.

(*a*) The QB fakes the run in one direction.

(*b*) Then the QB hands off to a back going the opposite direction.

Short First Step

When a quarterback wants to give a pulling lineman room to move along the line of scrimmage, he can take a short slide step from his exchange position to create space quickly between himself and the line of scrimmage (figure 3.15). On the snap, the quarterback slides the foot nearest the line of scrimmage back from the line of scrimmage about six inches. The second step is a normal step with the other foot. The six inches gained using this method is extremely helpful on traps or counter plays where guards or tackles pull. The maneuver takes some practice time but is an important skill for any quarterback to master, as the feet have a way of getting tangled when linemen are moving one way and the quarterback another.

Figure 3.15

A short slide step moves the QB away from the LOS quickly, giving the linemen room to block.

The first step in this action is with the upfield foot, and the distance of the farthest foot from the line of scrimmage is whatever the stance position allows. Generally this is fewer than 18 inches. When the slide step (using the deepest set foot in the stance) is used, the clearance distance can be as much as two feet, depending on the length of the drop step.

CHAPTER 4

RUNNING THE BALL

Run the ball and you win! At least that's what many people with football intuition most likely would say, and there is some degree of validity to this theory. For one thing, a solid running game allows the team that's winning to use more time, which may influence the final outcome. If you have the football, your opponent is less likely to score. An effective running attack also can help maintain good field position, which is a huge element in winning a game. The quarterback's monumental contribution to a team's ground game is exhibited in every running play.

The quarterback must understand the theory behind the running game if he is to have a chance for success. A running attack can only transpire if sound decisions are made as to when, where, and how to use the running game. The running package should complement the pass offense and vice versa. For the ground attack to best serve an offense, I suggest the following:

1. Run the football in a given game on all downs at least once.
2. Occasionally call for a run play in a definite pass situation.
3. Use a run play that complements the passing action being used most often in a specific contest.
4. Do not let personnel substitutions tip the defense as to whether a run or a pass is coming.
5. Whenever possible, do not let the clock or the score dictate a run or pass call.
6. Execute running plays from the same formations used to pass.

These six guidelines will escalate the value and productivity of the total offense by forcing the other team to defend or at least respect a running attack with some degree of preparation. Point number 2, above all others, is the heart of successful logic with regard to blending the pass and run.

Remember any play will work if it is sound in design, executed correctly, enough practice time is spent on its development, and the personnel fit the play. Each play has its own philosophy and characteristics. Good teams are productive offensively at something, but few excel using a large number of plays. Find two or three plays that you can count on consistently, and build the rest of the attack around those plays.

© G. Newman Lowrance

▪ The running game requires precision, teamwork, and solid execution.

Because the idea of almost all plays is to score a touchdown, common sense tells us it's not the number of plays an offense gets off; it's how well they are run. As in all other aspects of offensive football, the quarterback is the defining and influencing factor regardless of the nature of the running attack employed.

Running the football effectively requires precision, explosion at the point of attack, and solid execution with exact timing. When quality talent is added to the mix, the football will find its way to the end zone more often than not. Like the effectiveness of a passing attack, the success of the running game depends on the practice time allowed, coaching expertise, and the skill of the quarterback.

Chapters 2 and 3 discussed quarterback fundamentals in the areas of stance, footwork, and exchange. This chapter explores in more detail the basics for the signal caller in the running game and presents common running plays.

For a team to have a successful running game, the quarterback must consistently exhibit these key fundamentals:

- Appropriate stance. Feet are parallel or semiparallel. Weight is evenly distributed on both feet, with the toes pointed slightly inward. The buttocks are down, back is straight, and knees are bent slightly. The arms are bent at the elbow, just enough to allow a 12-inch ride with the hands under the center as the center gets off the line of scrimmage. The shoulders are rounded forward, and the thumbs touch at the second knuckle.

- Head and eyes. Before the snap, the quarterback should move his head from left to right, then return to a straight ahead position. On the snap, the quarterback's head and eyes look straight ahead. His chin is lifted to enable upfield eye focus and concentration.

- Eyeballing defensive alignment. As he approaches the line of scrimmage, the quarterback should confirm the number of players in the box (tight end to tight end), as well as their alignment. He also should measure the depth of the linebackers and count how many there are.

- Gripping the football. On all running plays, both hands of the quarterback should be on the ball in front-to-back position (see chapter 3). The football is carried near the body, with the nose of the ball up until the handoff procedure begins. While running, the quarterback carries the ball close to his belly button, which allows arm and hand fluidity.

- The handoff. There should be no body contact with the ball carrier. The quarterback places the football into the midsection of the runner at belly button level. The quarterback ought to reach with both hands until the ball touches the midsection of the ball carrier, at which point the hand nearest the ball carrier's abdomen comes off first.

- Angle of the quarterback's path. The quarterback's angle needs to be such that the quarterback does not get overextended. However, there must be enough room for the ball carrier to cut at a slight angle in the direction of the quarterback's exchange position. The first step of the angle must project the second step and so on to enable an appropriate mesh.

- Carrying out the fake. In the running game, carrying out the fake is most important. The opponent must not know who has the ball after the handoff until the quarterback has taken two steps. The quarterback uses his body either to hide the ball if he has it or to fool the defense into thinking he has the ball if he doesn't have it. A low profile helps hide the ball from the opposition.

Attack Strategies

Ground attacks are broken down into segments, and each attack can play a part in the total running game package. To have a complete running scheme, most systems advocate short-, normal-, and long-yardage plays. Within these packages, it is conceivable to have an option play, some form of draw, sweep, trap, dive, or counter. Rushing yards also can be accumulated through bootleg plays or unplanned scramble action plays. Although the quarterback's involvement in the run game is somewhat basic, it is critical to the success of every play, even more so with some specific plays.

Short-yardage plays should be divided into plays suitable for less than one yard and plays suitable for fewer than three yards. Because the defensive alignment tends to be tighter for less than one yard situations, some short-yardage plays are more appropriate for these situations. Plays selected to acquire less than one yard are the QB sneak and the FB smash (figure 4.1). Both of these plays may feature wedge blocking and are designed to go in a straight line straight ahead.

The quarterback's role is to get everyone lined up correctly and off on the cadence. He should focus on the quarterback–center exchange. On a short-yardage play, an exchange mishap becomes a disaster. Using a quick count generally helps the play.

Figure 4.1

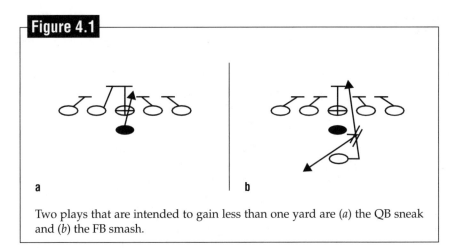

a   b

Two plays that are intended to gain less than one yard are (*a*) the QB sneak and (*b*) the FB smash.

These plays require linemen splits to be reduced to six inches or fewer, preventing or slowing defensive penetration. The line needs to crowd the ball by getting up on the line of scrimmage as much as possible. The front five must get off on the count and establish upfield movement along the front to create a new line of scrimmage. When the linemen create movement upfield, there is more room for the quarterback to execute the play. Blockers need to lower their profiles more than normal to meet the submarine charge of defenders. Guards and tackles must step first with their inside feet, using a shortened step approach. The inside arm is extended in a punching fashion at the base of the near number of the opponent. Remember, however, that this is zone blocking, so the blockers fire out to an area rather than at a specific player.

When trying to gain up to three yards, use one of the following strategies:

- Fake inside and go outside.
- Run option to beat pinch.
- Use straight-ahead plays.
- Power off tackle or iso power inside.

Faking inside and going outside involves a dive fake to one back and a pitch to another (figure 4.2). This action tends to make defensive linebackers commit quickly to the inside, temporarily freezing pursuit. The better the fake, the better the play. The play can be base blocked with pull and fill. The idea of the inside–go outside concept is that it holds the inside linebacker long enough to allow the play to develop outside.

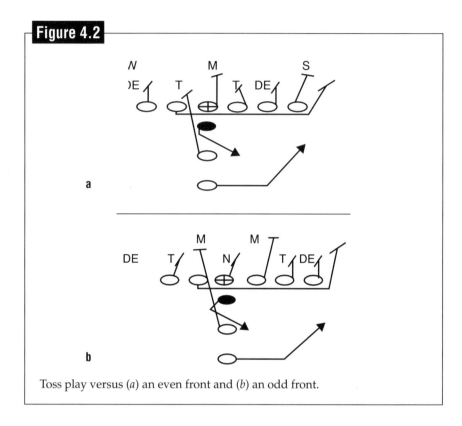

Figure 4.2

Toss play versus (*a*) an even front and (*b*) an odd front.

Quarterback's objective: Poise and smart ballhandling.

The option play overcomes the advantage the defense creates when it pinches. As the defensive front commits inside, the play quickly develops outside. Straight ahead running plays apply the principle that the shortest distance to a spot is a straight line. These plays also are used in normal situations.

Only a limited number of running plays can be classified as long-yardage plays. The most universally used plays for acquiring large chunks of real estate are draws, sweeps, traps, and counters. Reverses and other gadget (trick) plays in long-yardage situations usually are not effective.

Option

All option plays put tremendous pressure on a defense because the nature of the play is so radically different from all other aspects of offense. By far, the most common defense versus the option is to assign defenders to potential ball carriers. This strategy is in direct contrast with hole, area, contain, and lane support defenses that are the foundation of all defenses today.

The option can be run in normal situations or in short-yardage situations. Running the option to gain fewer than three yards places tremendous pressure on the defense because if they pinch or blitz, pursuit or flow becomes nonexistent. The option play in short-yardage or goal line situations is simple and generally most effective.

Two option plays that are effective in short-yardage or goal line situations are dive and load (figure 4.3). In both plays, the quarterback has to key only one defender to determine pitch or keep once the fake to the fullback has been made. The option play can be run from various backfield sets; figure 4.3 depicts the play from the I formation.

Figure 4.3

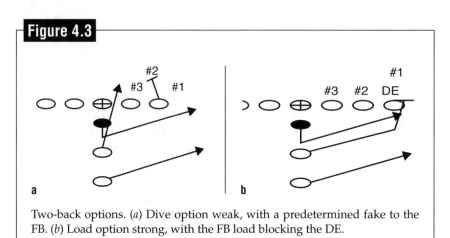

Two-back options. (*a*) Dive option weak, with a predetermined fake to the FB. (*b*) Load option strong, with the FB load blocking the DE.

In the option, the quarterback attacks, getting a commitment out of the last defender in the tight end to tight end imaginary box on or off the line of scrimmage. The quarterback ought to attack the upfield, or inside, shoulder of this defensive player. The blocking count system allows the rules to apply regardless of the defensive front. Because the quarterback options the last man on the line of scrimmage (number 1), the number 2 defender in the box belongs to the tight end or tackle, depending on the defensive formation. The number 3 defender in the box is picked up by the next lineman, and so on.

The quarterback uses an open-step, front-out technique on these plays. The quarterback should assume a football position as he steps into the pitch itself.

Quarterback's objective: Be athletic and smart.

Upfield Option

There are many forms of option plays, but unless an offense rallies its thrust around the single read option play, it must commit to a much more time-consuming and prepared option offense. For most offenses, the single option serves best as a complementary play in the attacks of a more traditional offense.

The single read option takes less time to perfect and has a lower turnover risk than the double or triple option. The single read option focuses on a single defender, with the quarterback making the decision to keep or pitch. Usually the man being optioned is the last defender on the line of scrimmage, who is likely to be the contain guy. The quarterback must take a path to attack the inside, or upfield, shoulder of this defender. If the defender commits himself to the quarterback, the quarterback pitches to the running back. If the defender commits to the running back, the quarterback keeps the football and turns upfield.

An option toss progresses from a two-handed grip to a one-handed tumbled pitch. While in the pitching mode, the quarterback should bend his knees slightly, as if sitting down, and pitch. The quarterback's eyes must be focused on the man he is optioning while his peripheral vision locates the running back in case he has to pitch the football. The play can be executed to the strong or weak side of the formation (figure 4.4).

The running back must maintain a distance of 4 1/2 to 5 yards from the quarterback and be in his vision. This relationship helps the quarterback's pitch as he is concentrating on the defensive action confronting him.

Quarterback's objective: Correct read and good pitch.

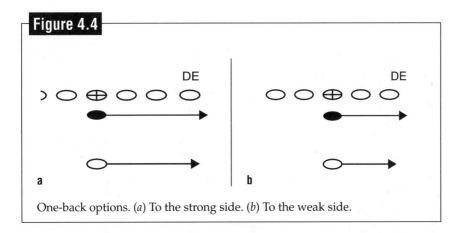

One-back options. (*a*) To the strong side. (*b*) To the weak side.

Off-Tackle Isolation Play

The isolation play involves blocking down or inside, with the linemen to the call side, and kicking out at the point of attack with a lead back (figure 4.5). The power inside isolation play features base blocking, with a lead back attacking the play-side linebacker. The center, if uncovered, blocks the most dangerous down linemen to the play side. The quarterback's role is to take the appropriate angle to handoff, make a good solid exchange, and carry out the fake.

Quarterback's objective: Good ballhandling and fake to hold defensive end or outside linebacker.

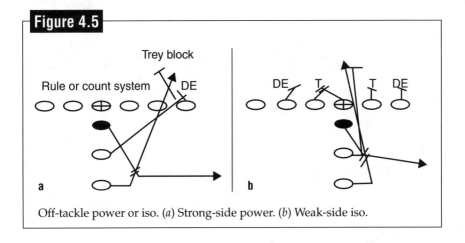

Off-tackle power or iso. (*a*) Strong-side power. (*b*) Weak-side iso.

Dive

The dive is one of the simplest yet yielding plays in the game. Since the inception of football in the late 1800s, the dive play has been explosive. Quickness is the heart and soul of making the play effective. Linemen must get off the ball quickly, and running backs must hit the line of scrimmage in high gear.

In a dive play, the running back breaks off the buttocks of the blocker at the point of attack (figure 4.6). The linemen move in a north and south direction (vertically), enabling a seam or soft spot in the defensive front. Base or man blocking is used. Above all else, linemen need to keep their shoulders square to the line of scrimmage and maintain a solid, low football position while executing their blocks. The offensive linemen target the defenders above the waist, about at the base of the numbers. The center, guards, and tackle should split as much as they can get away with. Ideally the center and play-side guard will be two to three feet apart, and the guard and play-side tackle will be three to four feet apart. The quarterback should give the ball off as deep in the backfield as he can, giving the running back time to read the blocks of the linemen.

Quarterback's objective: Look the ball into the back's exchange point and carry out the fake.

Figure 4.6

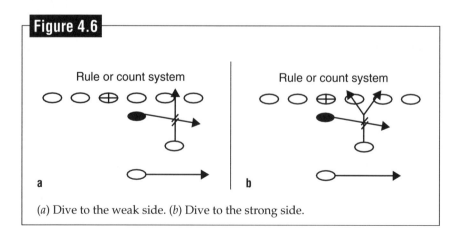

(*a*) Dive to the weak side. (*b*) Dive to the strong side.

Draw

Without a doubt, the biggest running play in football is the draw. By biggest, I mean the most explosive or potential yard-achieving play. Therefore, it is a strong play to call in long-yardage situations. It also can be used successfully anywhere on the field. The draw is more productive if used in conjunction with the quarterback's passing drop action and if the quarterback's draw action mirrors his passing drop.

There are several kinds of draw plays, and any of them will be successful if executed properly. The key to the draw is for the field general and running back to make their moves look like a pass play to throw the defense off the scent. A good pass rush from the defensive front helps by creating those most important rush lanes.

The one thing a defense can do to take the draw play away from an offense is to blitz into it. The quarterback has to check away from the draw when he senses a blitz coming. A defense that fills all the gaps (no two-gap defense) can make it difficult for an offense to get the draw play started. To boost the play's success, run it in a nonblitz situation. Remember, the draw is slow and delayed at its inception, so the defense can overwhelm the play with pressure in the A and B lanes, located between center/guard/tackle. However, in normal situations (a three- or four-man rush by the defense), the draw play is hard to stop.

Only on option and bootleg plays does the quarterback's execution require similar precision. Remember, a draw play looks like a pass to the defensive rushers, so they are in rush lanes to the quarterback. All the offensive linemen have to do is show pass with their setup drop and then turn the rusher. The offensive linemen then stay with the rushers until the running back has cleared the line of scrimmage. After he gets the football, the running back simply accelerates to daylight.

The three-step draw, five-step draw, sprint draw, and lead draw are four popular draw plays that are consistently productive (figure 4.7). A team should use the draw play that best fits its offense. For example, a drop-back passing team is more likely to use the three- or five-step draw. A sprint or roll-out team might choose the sprint draw.

Figure 4.7

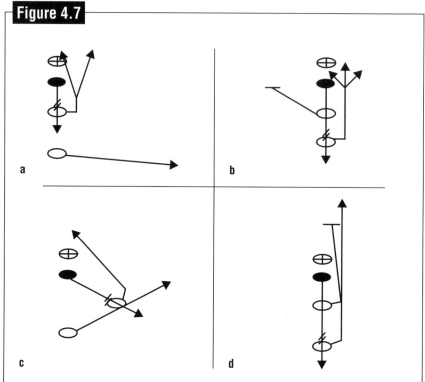

a

b

c

d

Draw plays. (*a*) Three-step draw to FB. (*b*) Five-step draw to TB. (*c*) Sprint draw. (*d*) Lead draw.

Quarterback's objective: Make the drop look like a pass and carry out the fake.

The techniques involved for each position when executing the draw play are critical to ensure success. The guards and tackles flash quick set-pass protection by throwing their hands into the defenders and dropping their outside feet, then taking short steps—not more than one yard in depth. They should stay low and maintain contact, turning rushers the way they want to go. They ride the rushers past the ball carrier, keeping their feet moving and losing ground.

The center uses the same technique as the guards and tackles, except he assumes a more squared-up position on his defender until the rusher chooses a pass rush side. Once the rusher commits, the center rides him past the ball carrier.

The running back steps to the play side (normally the right side). He shows his pass protection stance and arm action. For the handoff, he lifts his inside arm and takes the exchange. He should not move forward until the ball is secured and he has chosen a running lane. Then he runs to daylight, normally to the gap to the right or left side of the center. At times, the B or C gap will open up for the runner.

The receivers assume their maximum splits and release to the outside. They run as if on a pass route for three to five yards, then break down and block defenders covering using the inside position block. If the coverage is man to man, they continue their pass routes and take the defenders deep.

The quarterback takes his normal drop, carrying the football at the base of his numbers. He keeps his head and eyes upfield to influence the opponent's secondary. He hands off the football to the running back at the set position, then carries out the fake as if it was a pass play. To sell the fake, he keeps his upfield shoulder turned away from the line of scrimmage.

All players involved in blocking make the quarterback's job easier and the play more effective when they execute correctly. The idea for the blockers is to sell pass, then run block. It's the selling that the play is a pass that makes it effective.

Sweep

The sweep (figure 4.8) is the one play in football that combines power and finesse. There is both short-yardage and big-play potential with the sweep. This play is complex, as it involves precise timing and coordination between blockers and the ball carrier. A team must commit a lot of practice time to perfect this play because it won't be successful unless all players do their parts in sequence. Blockers need to remember four major points:

1. Allow no penetration by defenders.
2. Knock the contain man down.
3. Aggressively block primary force to allow running back to cut inside or out.
4. Prevent back-side pursuit from running down the play.

For the sweep, the back-side tackle steps with his inside foot and peels. The back-side guard and center cut off of the defenders on or off of them. The onside guard pulls and blocks his primary force.

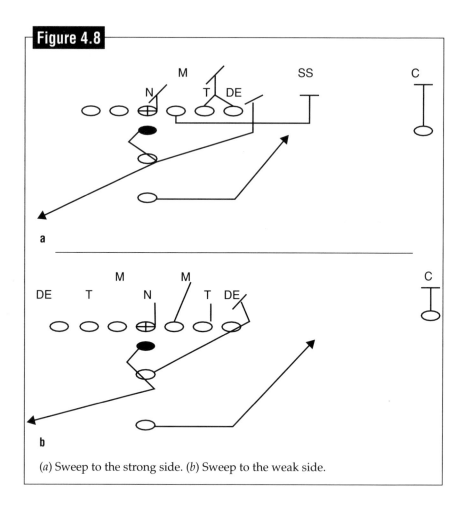

(a) Sweep to the strong side. (b) Sweep to the weak side.

The onside tackle blocks the man on or off of him. The tight end plays trey or doubles down. The onside wide receiver stack blocks the man covering him. The running back catches the toss 5 1/2 yards deep, squares up at the tight end position, and runs off the block of the pulling guard. The quarterback reverse pivots, dead pitches the ball, and seals the back side. He needs to make sure the pitch is soft, number high, and in front of the running back. The fullback leads and knocks the contain man down.

When the defense adjusts to the play based on coverage, the primary force may change the assignments of the wide receiver and pulling guard. The guard now blocks the corner, assuming he is the primary force and the safety is not. Instead of blocking the corner, the wide receiver works to a collision course with the safety. To help the wide receiver get to the safety quickly, he should reduce the distance to the formation if time permits, before the play begins. If there is not enough time, he must release at a flat angle to ensure he can get to the safety.

Quarterback's objective: A good pitch.

Traps and Counters

Traps and counters are somewhat maverick to any other aspect of the offense, but they serve their purposes.

There is no other play in football that can more effectively discourage a defender's pass rush than the trap. It also works well against defenders who are physical players and tend not to use instinct or reactionary techniques. A trap play can use many actions, as far as the running back is concerned, but the most important thing is that the running back runs with the football as close to the trap block as possible (figure 4.9). The linemen need to influence the defensive linemen being trapped with either a release away from the direction the trapper is coming or by flashing a pass protection look to encourage the rush and then blocking the first man off the line of scrimmage, away from the direction the trapper is coming.

Quarterback's objective: A perfect handoff.

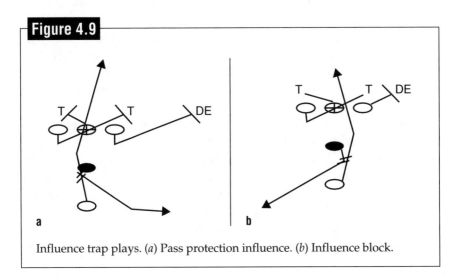

Figure 4.9

a

b

Influence trap plays. (*a*) Pass protection influence. (*b*) Influence block.

Figure 4.10

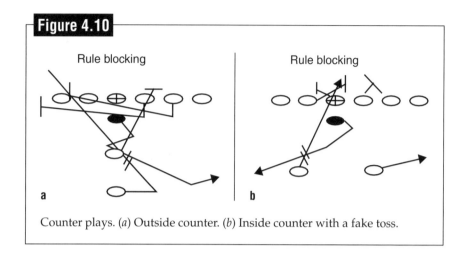

Counter plays. (*a*) Outside counter. (*b*) Inside counter with a fake toss.

Counter plays (figure 4.10) are designed to influence defensive pursuit in a given direction, allowing the play to develop in the opposite direction. Most counter plays are slow to develop.

Zone

Originated in the early 1990s, the zone play was developed to counter defensive alignments and tactics. In the '70s and '80s, strategies such as scraping linebackers, plugging inside gaps, line variation stunts and blitzing all were perfected and used by defenses. Defensive schemes during this period gave many running attacks fits because the quick flow overwhelmed wide running plays.

To combat this evolution, offensive coaches created a play that picked it all up and returned the execution advantage to the offense. Today, the zone play is popular and remains effective. The only negative with zone play is the amount of teaching time required to perfect it.

Because the zone differs greatly in concept, philosophy, and technique from traditional plays, it can demand as much as 25 percent of run offense teaching time. The zone play (figure 4.11) features area blocking on the move rather than conventional man or combination-type blocking. A lineman involved in zone play becomes responsible for blocking one gap or man to his right or left (what used to be called a reach technique) while on the move. A technique that resembles a pull technique is used to accomplish this maneuver.

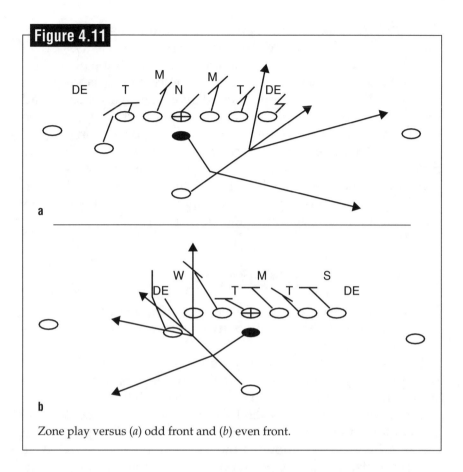

Zone play versus (*a*) odd front and (*b*) even front.

Today, the term used in the execution of play is "bucket step," which is a drop and widening step followed by a crossover in the direction of play.

When all linemen are moving in the same direction in this play, all gaps and defensive front alignments are accounted for. The moving wall effectively blocks every conceivable defensive pattern.

The tailback or running back is given the option of going one of three places on this play. Once he has the ball, he can continue outside, drive straight at the tackle gap, or cut back inside to the guard gap. Some offenses have inside and outside zone plays. I advocate one, with the option to go inside or out.

The quarterback's role in the zone play is simple yet most important. He must front out with a lead step, angled in the direction of the exchange point. His eye focus and path are directly to the handoff spot. The exchange point is a minimum of six yards deep, directly behind the offensive tackle to the play side. He uses a one-handed handoff as he stretches to the maximum. If the play is going to the quarterback's right, he uses a left-handed handoff; if it goes to his left, he uses a right-handed give. The quarterback's lead foot at the exchange point must be the same (left or right) as the hand he uses to give the football to the running back. Carrying out the fake after the exchange is critical to the success of the zone play. Also a play action pass can be tied to it. The signal caller must keep both hands on the ball and close to his body until the one-handed reach handoff takes place. His play-side shoulder stays closed to the line of scrimmage as much as possible during and after the exchange.

Cutback

Created to beat overpursuing linebackers and linemen, the cutback play penalizes a defense for mobility in general and chasing the action of a ball carrier in particular.

Initially the cutback play (figure 4.12) looks like a zone play, with the ball given off deep and the running back creating the stretch, looking like he is going outside. As with the zone play, the quarterback uses a one-handed handoff and gives the ball deep. His angle on the cutback play, however, is to the B gap, between the guard and tackle, allowing the back to cut back to the onside A gap or offside B or C gap. In other words, the path of the running back is almost the same as the one he takes in zone, but the field general must compensate for the possibility of the ball carrier cutting back. Therefore, there should be good separation (one yard) between the quarterback and running back at the exchange point.

As when executing the zone play, the quarterback takes a front-out lead step, deep toward the give spot. The ball must be secured with both hands until the exchange begins.

To fake, the quarterback stretches his path deep and wide after the exchange. He keeps his back to the line of scrimmage for two seconds or until the running back has crossed the line of scrimmage.

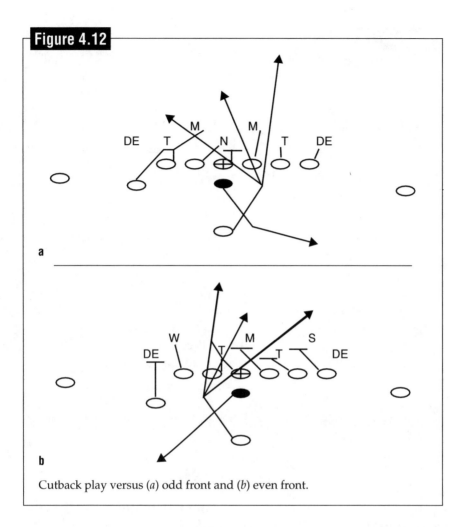

Figure 4.12

a

b

Cutback play versus (*a*) odd front and (*b*) even front.

Bootleg

A bootleg play (figure 4.13) is in itself a counter, but the action of the play is designed to penalize not only defenders lined up in the box but the secondary as well. The main feature of the play is that the quarterback is the ball carrier. The play can be run with or without a guard pulling. With the guard pulling, the play relies totally on the fake. If the guard doesn't pull, the contain man to the called side must be fooled by the makeup of the play and commit inside. Bootlegs usually are run plays but can also lead to a pass.

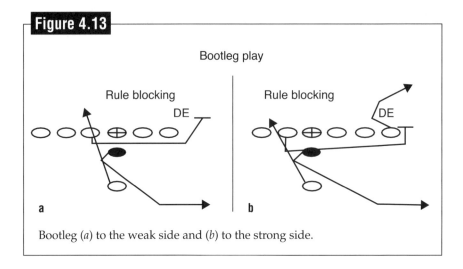

Figure 4.13

Bootleg play

Rule blocking · Rule blocking

Bootleg (*a*) to the weak side and (*b*) to the strong side.

The quarterback's mission is to make a good reach fake and then follow the path of the man he faked to for a step with his head and eyes. His next assignment is to place the football between his hip, farthest from the line of scrimmage, and his abdomen, riding the ball for three to five yards.

Quarterback's objective: A great head–eye fake and to hide the ball.

Scrambles

Scramble plays are broken plays. In a scramble, the quarterback spills out of the pocket after he has dropped back to pass. This play has no structure or design; therefore, it is unpredictable at the beginning. For the defense, it's a nightmare to defend and stop. A quick quarterback can play havoc with the pass rush by spilling out. Who can forget John Elway and Rich Gannon from professional football, Nebraska's Eric Crouch, or Virginia Tech's former standout Michael Vick when it comes to scrambling?

Scrambling is a secondary reaction that the quarterback adopts when he sees a quick pass rush, when he is flushed out of the pocket after he sets up, when all the receivers are covered, or when the secondary changes coverage late and destroys the key.

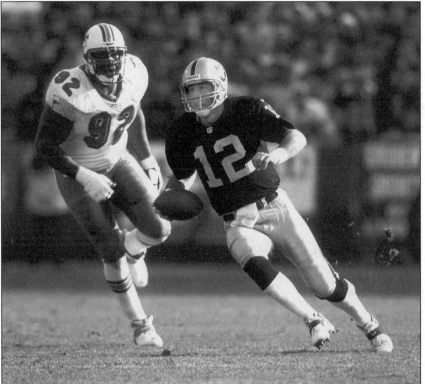

© Newsport Photography

■ A defensive pass rush is not a problem for a quarterback who can scramble. Rich Gannon is one of the best at spilling out of the pocket and turning a broken play into a gain.

A good way to teach a quarterback to scramble is to put him with the linemen when they are practicing pass protection. After a predetermined time of three seconds or so, have the quarterback scramble on the blast of a horn. Because this explosive play is not part of the play book, it has little direction to itself and no predetermined blocking pattern. This is why it is almost impossible to perfect in practice. However, offensive players should adhere to a few rules when a scramble play develops. Blockers should do the following:

- Reject the instinct to block someone illegally, such as from behind.
- Anticipate that the quarterback may cut back in their direction.

- Move upfield and not be cheerleaders and stand around.
- Beware of hitting late or piling on when the play is over.

There is a drill that helps educate the entire team as to what to do when the scramble starts. When the scramble develops, most of the offense will have their backs to the quarterback and won't realize the scramble is on. Therefore, notification is helpful. One word will suffice to let others know what has happened. Choose an action word that has a catchy meaning. Words that seem to work well are "geronimo" or "avalanche." The quarterback yells this word a couple of times as he begins his escape. The quarterback will execute the drill by running around and changing direction. The linemen react and block as well as they can.

Quarterback's objective: Feel the pressure and react accordingly.

CHAPTER 5

READS IN RUN SITUATIONS

Just as with every other aspect of the quarterback position, improvement in reading the defense is possible with a commitment to a good course of action. There are several ways to help a quarterback increase his functional ability with respect to reads in the running game. Quarterbacks must perform film study of their opponents, repeat plays in practice that provide realistic looks, and regularly review defined gamelike pressures. The only way a quarterback can get better at any aspect of football is to amass many repetitions of the very thing that he is trying to perfect, especially in run reads. A quarterback's comfort zone has to be expanded in this facet of his job, and only hard work will make it happen. Confidence and knowhow stem from repetition. Bringing about constant positive reads in the run game for the quarterback is related to both preparation and instincts.

Even though the signal caller's instincts with respect to run reads are, for the most part, natural attributes, refinements can be made. Preparation includes understanding and analyzing; mastering these qualities has no restrictions or limits for the quarterback. He can be as good at recognizing defensive roadblocks to his running game as he desires. Preparation comes down to a matter of commitment. "I have met the enemy and he is me,"—so it is with the role of today's quarterback and his run reads! He alone can restrict or expand his functional ability with this most important part of offensive football.

If you really look, you will see! That's how it is when identifying the defense's game strategy. A quarterback's job while directing a running play is to focus his attention primarily on the defensive players in the imaginary box directly in front of him, tight end to tight end. This assessment begins when the quarterback leaves the huddle and concludes when the ball comes up on the exchange. It is extremely important for the quarterback to determine how many defensive linemen are in the box and the number of linebackers. With this information, the quarterback can identify the bubbles in the defensive alignment, which is critical for the success of the upcoming play. The quarterback then classifies the nature of the front and the strength of the alignment. It is important for him to gather most of this data before arriving at the line of scrimmage or within five seconds after reaching the exchange position. The time allowed to get the play off (25 seconds in college and 30 in high school) limits what the quarterback can deduce, but he can aid his cause through his perceptions.

Determining Fronts

Studying film and scouting reports help prepare the quarterback for recognizing fronts, line stunts, and blitzes. This helps the signal caller get a jump on a potential change of play or blocking calls if he makes them. If the quarterback is not required to determine blocking calls, he nonetheless can relay the alignment to the center or whomever makes these calls. Usually when the quarterback does not make blocking calls, which is the case in many systems, his mission is to let his offensive linemen and backs know if the defense is odd, even, or some form of gap. Most defensive fronts are not head up but shaded. Nonetheless, classification of odd, even, or gap should be made by the quarterback to help linemen with their assignments (figure 5.1).

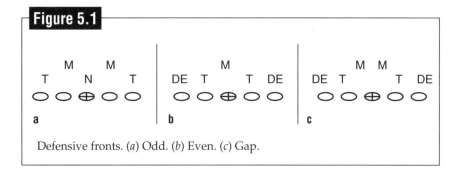

Figure 5.1

Defensive fronts. (*a*) Odd. (*b*) Even. (*c*) Gap.

Regardless of whether blocking calls are made by the quarterback or he just identifies the defensive front, this information is barked to his teammates before the start of the cadence (see chapter 2). A potential late blitz should be recognized by the quarterback to aid the linemen and backs in blocking appropriately when possible. Alerting the offensive front loud and clear twice assists in clarification and identification. Along with classifying the alignment, the signal caller should recognize and identify the strength of the defensive front and backers according to the number of players in the box on each side of the ball. He should holler or point with both hands what he has recognized, first to the left side of the offensive formation then to the right. One thing the quarterback must not do is to stare or concentrate his eyes at a designated hole where the play is to be run.

Assessing Matchups and Blocking Patterns

As a football game evolves, information on defensive personnel or alignments needs to be assessed and adjustments made accordingly. If, for example, a given play is not working, there is a reason—either there are poor blocking matchups or the defense is doing something to shut down what the offense is trying to execute. Determine where the problem is and decide if it can be remedied. Normally, if a player or players are unable to defeat a defender in the blocking scheme, going the other way with play selection is recommended.

Sometimes, however, changing the technique being used can help. A blocking pattern can be changed to give the blockers a better chance at success. Switching from man blocking to trap, double team, gap, scoop, turn back, influence, reach, cross blocking, or some other form of blocking might do the trick. The key is to provide the best possible thrust at the point of attack, allowing maximum opportunity for achievement. Sometimes blocking a front and linebackers a specific way changes an ineffective play into a productive one.

A defensive end playing extremely wide may not be conducive to man blocking (figure 5.2a). Changing to cross blocking (figure 5.2b) becomes more effective.

Figure 5.2

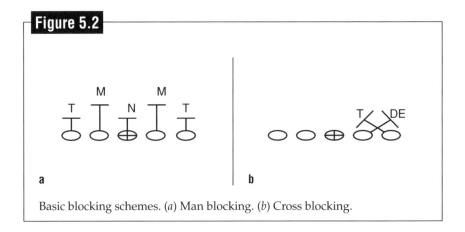

Basic blocking schemes. (*a*) Man blocking. (*b*) Cross blocking.

A running back can be added to the blocking pattern mix to turn an ineffective play into a productive one (figure 5.3). When there is no back blocking, the quarterback's fake is most important.

Figure 5.3

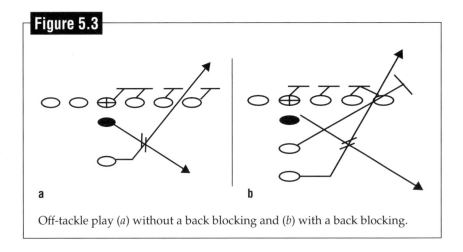

Off-tackle play (*a*) without a back blocking and (*b*) with a back blocking.

Wedge and zone blocking are two other solid methods for dealing with an extra-tough defender or an alignment that seems to defeat the blocking design (figures 5.4 and 5.5). Both wedge and zone blocking tend to handle either of these problems easier because the emphasis changes from an individual's ability to move a defender to a group concept of attacking one, two, or more defensive players at the point of attack. The quarterback must recognize the advantage or disadvantage of various blocking schemes if the play is to have the best chance for success. After this, he can use an automatic call to change the play to one that features advantageous blocking. Another way the quarterback can positively influence the play is to call for a blocking scheme or allow an assigned lineman to.

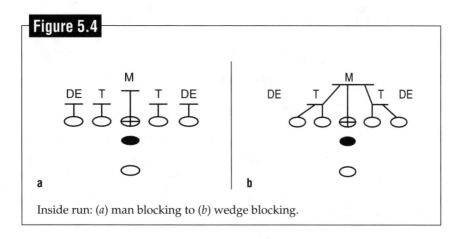

Figure 5.4

a

b

Inside run: (*a*) man blocking to (*b*) wedge blocking.

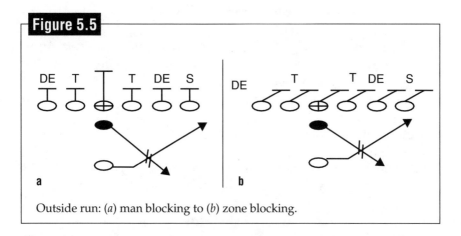

Figure 5.5

a

b

Outside run: (*a*) man blocking to (*b*) zone blocking.

So far, the emphasis of assessing and changing blocking assignments has been confined to switching methods because the defense is overwhelming or at least handling the offense at a specific place along the front. Understand, however, that most run plays are built to defeat both defensive alignments or any form of blitz.

It is most important for the quarterback to determine where and how successful plays are functioning. If an offense has created an advantage with its personnel or method of blocking, flaunt it! A cardinal rule is to stay with good plays until the defense takes them away. Too often this does not occur, as teams tend to beat themselves by not calling on enough of those plays that are proved to be good. The quarterback should keep a mental account of which plays are working and which are not. This is valuable not only for play selection but for audibles.

Look for Specific Techniques and Tendencies

The way a linebacker is positioned and his depth off the ball tell the quarterback a lot. A defensive player's weight distribution can also be a clue as to what the defense is about to do. A strong safety or corner also can provide a wealth of tip-off information on the nature of the defense. Stance, alignment, and visible pattern are giveaways as to who has primary support, potential blitz, and coverage responsibilities.

All defenses use favorite alignments and coverages versus various offensive formations, hash-mark, or down-and-distance situations. Knowledge of what the defensive tendency is in any situation is paramount to the success of the play not only for potential change of play but to better anticipate what the defense is going to do so that the play can be more efficiently blocked. A quarterback who has done his homework—studying scouting reports and analyzing videotape of opponents—usually is perceptive about recognizing defensive fronts.

Offensive linemen also ought to read the stance, alignment, and weight distribution of defensive linemen. This can be of great assistance in determining the blocking technique to be used. It might help linemen decide which foot steps first or the aiming point for a type of block. Being able to anticipate the intentions of the opponent is helpful and provides a blocking advantage.

Checking Off and Improvising

Once a quarterback has done all the sizing up he can do, he has two other missions before he starts the cadence: Get out of a bad play and check to a better play if he needs to. If a check is to be made, the rule of thumb is to choose a less complex play that will be better than the one originally called. To change to a more complicated play is asking for trouble. Changing a sweep or trap play to a dive is easy and less likely to lead to an assignment breakdown. Sweep and trap plays require a guard or guards to pull, and blocking the other linemen is far more involved than base-rule, blocking-type plays such as the dive.

Offensive players have only three to five seconds to absorb any change of play, so the more complicated the change, the greater the chance of error. If two, three, or four players have to switch assignments, the probability of mishap grows accordingly.

Courtesy of Don Read

▪ When changing the play at the line of scrimmage, the quarterback should switch to a less complex play than the one originally called.

A Lesson in Innovation

While coaching a high school team in Petaluma, California, I learned a lot about coaching football from a young quarterback named Nino Pedrini. His daring tactics and outstanding ability often made my job easy and very exciting.

Nino was also our punter. At a critical time during a big game, deep in our own territory, this talented and sometimes reckless 18-year-old, with the option to run or punt, started the play as run, stopped near the line of scrimmage, and punted the football. The ball carried 68 yards with no return! Our opponent had bad field position, and we were able to defend a much longer field.

Nino's daring exploits often provided wins for our team. The best thing at a given time is often the quarterback's innovation (or in this case, the punter–quarterback's innovation).

A second consideration the field general must get involved with is improvising, which can mean changing the formation on the line of scrimmage or simply running with the football himself. Both of these commonly used adjustments are the result of the quarterback's creativity and understanding what is the best thing to do in a bad situation. The following are typical improvisation situations:

- Changing formation, forcing the defense to alter secondary run support
- Spreading the defense to provide a more delayed run support
- Reacting to a quick defensive line pass rush and running
- Running a quarterback sneak if there is a late change in defensive alignment that might affect the play called
- Keeping the football instead of handing it off when the defense is stacked to defeat the predetermined play

For the most part, improvising relies on the instincts of the quarterback. It creates a better play at the last second than the one originally called.

Reads in run situations are totally in the hands of the quarterback. The coach can't make these decisions, nor can any of the other players. Mental preparation, instinct, and poise are a quarterback's primary resources. The quarterback alone is right or wrong when it comes to handling most challenges. Some athletes are gifted with the physical and mental traits necessary to execute and master these configurations. Signal callers who do not have these qualifications struggle to be effective in this very important part of their duties.

CHAPTER 6

DROPS AND SETUPS TO THROW

When drops and quarterback passing action are interwoven correctly into a system, productivity emerges. Timing and the relationship of the quarterback to the receiver are everything to a passing attack. Even more pertinent are the quarterback's setups as they relate to the pass protection being used. Careful and ongoing study of these components, appropriate drills, and allocation of practice time can ensure a sound, effective pass offense.

Gripping the football appropriately is critical (see chapter 7) because this affects the throwing action and prevents a fumble. The grip involves good finger spacing, with both hands establishing a balanced hold on the ball. The throwing hand has to be placed on the upper half of the football while the nonthrowing hand secures the base. The forefinger of the quarterback's throwing hand is placed at a comfortable angle toward the upper point of the ball. There should be about one finger width between the pigskin and the palm of the quarterback's throwing hand. The firm grip of the quarterback will show through his lack of turnovers and solid throwing delivery.

When the football arrives late or early to the receiver, there is a reason. Much of the time, it's because the quarterback's steps are wrong for the play. If the quarterback is under heavy pressure, using an alternate form of drop or setup will help. It is important to select the correct and most effective drop to provide timing to the pass play, depending on the quarterback's skills.

Regardless of the nature of the depth of drops, the quarterback's head alignment and eye focus are of major importance. Head and eyes not only should be used to locate targets but also serve to influence coverage while in the drop. Successful passers, particularly against zone coverage, are adept at freezing or moving people. Although all secondary players can be affected by the quarterback's head and eyes, the free safety or both safeties in a two-deep coverage can be swayed the most.

The first step of any drop, except the quick set, should involve looking either to the middle of the defense or to the opposite direction of where the throw is intended. Depending on the pattern being executed, during the second and third step, the same head and eye concentration needs to be exhibited.

Focus should come off and zero in on a primary receiver or key by the second step in a three-step drop, and by the third or fourth step in a five-step drop. Seven-step drops encourage the looking-away process to last until the fifth or sixth step.

Shotgun drops fall in the five-step technique or seven-step method, depending on the depth of the alignment and steps taken from the original shotgun formation. Half-roll and sprint-out actions do not require the looking-away process, as the concentration involves scanning the part of the field to which the ball will be thrown. This method is called reading the coverage, which contrasts to keying on one person.

When man coverage is recognized, the quarterback focuses on timing the throw rather than trying to move the coverage. For this reason, predetermining potential coverage is important, enabling the signal caller to concentrate on zone or man passing strategy.

In the final analysis, a team that doesn't use passing actions that mesh with the play called or skills of the offense has an extremely ineffective pass offense, period. The end result will be hurried throws, poor vision of the field, limited follow-through action and throwing off balance. Any of these flaws in an overall passing scheme can lead to one of three passing attack killers: sacks, incompletions, or interceptions.

All quarterbacks are born with or perfect specific skills related to the position. Setting up to pass the football ranks high as a needed asset. When a quarterback knows how to set up to pass, he is likely to be a good passer.

In reality, the forward pass begins not with the throw but with the drop action and all the mechanics that complement the setup. Today's quarterback cannot function as if he has two left feet.

Stance is where everything begins, as weight distribution and push off depend on correct stance. Stance, like exchange, is the subtle factor in all setups. If the quarterback's weight distribution in the stance is not back and on the push-off foot (left foot for right-handed passers), he will be slower in his drop and off balance. Knee bend, too, helps the first step push back, as a person can move faster when the push-off knee is bent slightly. A narrow-based stance is also helpful in accelerating the drop process because the closer the distance between the feet, the longer the first step can be, which is critical to the drop process. Another consideration is the stagger of the feet because when the push-off foot is back farther than the other foot, distance is gained from the line of scrimmage in the first step, as shown in figure 6.1.

Figure 6.1

The QB's first step should pull him away from the LOS.

Stationary Throwing and Passing on the Run

The feet position, weight distribution, and momentum process in passing differ greatly with drop and sprint actions. Stationary throwing and passing on the run require different techniques to provide accuracy and velocity to the football. That is why a quarterback needs to experience drills that perfect these skills.

In drop action that is designed to become stationary—whether it uses a quick set; three-, five-, or seven-step drop; play action; or half roll/sprint—the final foot plant serves two important purposes. First, it brakes the setup action. Second, it positions the back leg for the throwing process about to begin.

The final step in drops is the most important one (figure 6.2). The plant foot supplies the push forward through weight distribution transfer from back to front foot. The correct setting of the back foot, with knee bent to straight leg action, is what adds velocity to each pass.

Figure 6.2

For stationary passing, the last step is crucial. The QB's last step stops the setup action and prepares his back leg for the throwing action.

To brake consistently and appropriately, the last step of the drop comes down with that knee bent at about a 25-degree angle, although this can vary depending on body type. This position provides the coil or spring to push forward and change weight from back foot to front.

Throwing on the run, like stationary passing, demands correct foot placement in the final step. Stationary passing begins with planting the back foot, but when a quarterback is running with the football, throwing technique is the opposite—he throws off the front foot (figure 6.3).

Throwing on the move requires the passing action to begin on the lead, or upfield, foot. The quarterback must have good balance on the final step, be under control, and hold the ball higher to allow quicker delivery. The quarterback's weight is forward rather than back, placing him in his follow-through position at the beginning of his throwing action. There is no change of weight from back to front foot, as in stationary passing.

Figure 6.3

When throwing on the run, the QB throws off his front foot.

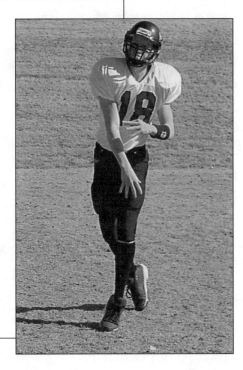

Choosing a Drop

There are four fundamental drops and three actions from which to throw the football: quick set, three step, five step, and seven step. In this chapter, we will compare each of these approaches and analyze the various drops and intricacies of each procedure. There are elements within the drops that have some things in common, but there is also uniqueness about each setup.

Quick Set

The quick set (figure 6.4) permits the quarterback to get the ball to a receiver almost instantly. Routes such as slant, hitch, swing, and pop all require the quick set drop. Pass routes that are fewer than five yards in depth or that take under two seconds to develop need to link up with quick set drops.

Figure 6.4

Quick set. The QB steps with his right foot, short steps with his left foot, then throws the ball.

When throwing to the left (if right handed), the quarterback drop steps with his right foot, short steps with his left foot, and throws. When throwing to the right, he does the opposite, stepping first with the left foot, then the right, and throws. Whether throwing to the left or to the right, the quarterback should bring the football to the top of his number or to shoulder level from the snap. The quarterback bypasses the securing phase of the throwing action (ball to the base of the numbers) so as not to slow release. The steps taken in the drop are short, as the emphasis is on getting the ball away quickly. The distance of the setup should not exceed 1 1/2 yards from the buttocks of the center.

Three-Step Drop

Like the quick set, the three-step drop is designed to get the ball off quickly. Patterns or routes that fit with the three-step drop are quick outs, short posts, curls fewer than 10 yards, short stops inside the plus 10-yard line, and shortened-up fades. Steve Young, the mobile quarterback for the San Francisco 49ers, maybe was the best ever at all short drops.

The depth of the three-step drop should be 3 1/2 to 5 yards. The quarterback carries the football in the drop at his numbers with both hands. The ball should be on its way as his back foot (right foot if right handed) hits the ground on the third step. The three-step drop uses the same step fundamentals as the quick set, except there are only three steps involved. If the quarterback is right handed, he steps with his right foot, then the left crosses over, then the right foot steps again (figure 6.5). When he is throwing to the left, his first step is to reach, then crossover, and finally reach. (Reach steps are longer strides that gather more distance than crossover steps.)

On the final step, he should open his front left hip to a 45-degree angle with the line of scrimmage, with the left shoulder and hip rotated to a semi-open position (figure 6.5d). The adjustment in the drop allows the throwing arm to come through faster. Visualize a hitter in baseball who uses an open stance, and you have the quarterback on his final step ready to throw quickly to his left.

Figure 6.5

The three-step drop.

(*a*) The QB steps with his right foot.

(*b*) He crosses over with his left foot.

(*c*) Then he steps again with his right foot.

(*d*) When he throws the ball, the QB's left shoulder and hip should be in a semi-open position.

Five-Step Drop

Because most passes are thrown using this drop technique, it's essential that the quarterback master the five-step drop. In football history, no one else was better at the five-step drop than Joe Montana, the all-time great San Francisco 49er superstar, or Drew Brees, a great quarterback for Purdue and the San Diego Chargers. The five-step drop is used to throw curls, delays, screens, crossing routes, and most multiple patterns. Most patterns that are more than 10 yards in depth upfield require the five-step drop. For patterns that take longer than 3.8 seconds to develop, it is recommended that the seven-step drop be used.

All aspects of the three-step drop need to be incorporated into the five-step drop, except there are two more steps involved. The stepping action is right-left-right-left-right for a right-handed quarterback. As in the three-step drop action, there are reach and crossover steps. The first step is reach, followed by crossover, reach, crossover, and reach (figure 6.6).

During the drop, the quarterback carries the ball somewhere between the base and top of his number. There is a tendency for quarterbacks to lower the ball below the numbers in this drop, and some even one hand the football. Carrying the ball too low or only in the passing hand is dangerous. More fumbles occur because of this lazy habit than any other factor in the quarterback's throwing procedure because the football is being held in a less secure position and is more vulnerable to pass rushers trying to strip it away.

The elbows of the quarterback should be pointed down toward the ground when he sets to throw the football. The quarterback should be constantly reminded of this fundamental, from junior high school through professional football.

Seven-Step Drop

The primary purpose of the seven-step drop is to put the quarterback farther from the line of scrimmage and pass rushers. However, it also allows the quarterback to see the secondary and receivers better. The seven-step drop should be used for slower-developing plays or deeper passes, normally 3.8- to 4.5-second pass plays. The seven-step drop ought to be used sparingly at the high school level unless the quarterback has exceptional arm strength or lacks the necessary height for adequate visibility. Seven-step drops normally feature routes or patterns that are 25 yards or deeper.

Figure 6.6

The five-step drop.

(*a*) The first, third, and last steps are reach steps.

(*b*) The second and fourth steps are crossover steps.

Step action for the seven-step drop is exactly like the five-step drop but with the addition of two extra steps. A right-handed passer follows a right-left-right-left-right-left-right drop pattern. The footwork pattern is similar to the three- and five-step drops, as there is reach, crossover, reach, crossover, reach, crossover, reach. The setup distance is 9 to 11 yards. Otto Graham, Terry Bradshaw, Joe Namath, Johnny Unitas, Bob Waterfield, and Norm Van Brocklin, as well as Chris Weinke, Florida State's all-time great, are among the best deep drop quarterbacks ever to play the game.

Half Roll

The half-roll action can be quite effective when incorporated for the right reasons. Theoretically, there are two vital advantages to half-roll setting up: to avoid inside or one-sided pressure and to put the quarterback closer to the side the throw will go to.

When pressure comes from an overpowering defensive pass rusher or rushers, the half roll can be used to hold the pressure in check. To get away from an overshifted alignment is another reason to employ the half roll (figure 6.7).

Figure 6.7

The half roll takes the QB away from pass rushers or an overshifted defensive alignment.

The setup position for the half roll begins behind one of the offensive tackles at the designated depth of five or seven steps, depending on the angle of drop, as it is in the drop-back setup. The final step requires a slightly shorter stride, which is true in all stationary setups. The quarterback's passing position changes the pash rusher's rush lanes. By altering the angles in which the rush comes, offensive linemen to the side of the setup now have a predetermined side to protect first.

On the back side, the blocker steps with his inside foot back and to the inside, creating a close off to the inside rush. The linemen away from the setup side turn their shoulders on the second step, placing the outside back at a 45-degree angle to the line of scrimmage. The only rush lane the defender then has is to the outside of the pass blocker, making the back-side rush run farther because of the bow or hinge created. Onside offensive linemen use the same protection procedure, as if the play were a drop back. The technique used should correlate to the drop-back depth action. For example, if normal five-step drop protection is slide and seven-step man, so should it be on the half-roll setups.

Shotgun

Hall of Fame quarterback Dan Fouts of the San Diego Chargers made the drop within the shotgun formation popular and productive. In the 1950s, Y. A. Tittle of the San Francisco 49ers was another great at throwing from the shotgun. More recently, Oklahoma's Josh Heupel fine-tuned the use of this formation. These quarterbacks took short and long drops from the gun alignment to time their throws with receivers and function within the protection scheme.

Shotgun depth corresponds to the five-step drop unless a drop is made from the gun to extend to a seven-step depth. When dropping from the shotgun, the quarterback's steps are exactly like those of five- or seven-step drops, except the steps are shorter because the quarterback is initially set back five yards.

Shotgun drops and actions are unique. Using the shotgun alignment has countless advantages, although some football experts will disagree. So-called West Coast offense advocates tend to frown on the use of shotgun because they think it delays the quarterback's ball release. The following are the primary advantages for using the shotgun formation:

- The quarterback can see the opponent's secondary better.
- The quarterback is in a better position to avoid the pass rush.
- The quarterback can find the throwing lanes more easily when he steps up.
- The quarterback has more time to throw.
- The offensive blockers can counter any quick unchecked pass rushes to the A or B gaps.
- Sight adjustment plays with receivers are more effective.

The quarterback depth should be about five yards from the football, although there are some quarterbacks who operate better a little deeper. A quarterback needs to align himself directly behind the center and assume a comfortable two-point football position (figure 6.8). His hands are out in front, slightly above his waist, to receive the football and provide a target for the snap. The quarterback has to see the center's ball release without concentrating on it so that he can take in the rushers and coverage.

Figure 6.8

Shotgun position. The QB sets up about five yards behind the ball, stands in a comfortable two-point football position, and holds his hands near his waist to give the center a target.

Working intensely with a center will improve the exchange process and its accuracy. Practices should incorporate drills that allow the center and quarterback to practice from the shotgun. Putting a bag or player in front of the center makes the drill realistic and forces the center to block something or someone while centering the football. Keeping charts on practice accuracy can also motivate the center. Many say that few centers can make the short snap required in the shotgun, but my experience tells me this is not valid. With practice, a center can perfect this skill and become consistent in making short snaps. The center needs to visualize the quarterback's hands and keep his buttocks down while projecting the football through his legs. The ball needs to be centered at a speed that is manageable for the quarterback to allow hand–eye coordination to kick in.

Sprint Out or Rollout

The sprint-out or rollout procedure is similar to the half roll. The main purpose of the sprint out or roll out is for the quarterback to escape the normal inside pass rush and acquire a more isolated position from which to throw the football. Other reasons for using the sprint out or rollout are the increased amount of time the quarterback has to pass the football and the fact that the quarterback is closer to the receivers who will be catching the ball. The sprint out or rollout also creates defensive pursuit or flow, slowing down the direct pass rush and setting up counteraction plays.

The quarterback either uses a front-out technique and sprints out (figure 6.9) or uses the reverse pivot and rolls out (figure 6.10), depending on the quarterback's preference and the blocking scheme. Sprint-out action is a faster way to get the quarterback outside, while the rollout relies on either deception (a back faking) or provides the blockers more time to position themselves, particularly the player blocking the defense's contain man so that the quarterback can get outside.

No matter which action is used, the quarterback must get quick depth to at least 5 1/2 yards. The drop angle needs to intercept the imaginary foot-plant position of the running back (right foot if going right, left foot if going left), lined up directly behind the quarterback at 5 1/2 yards. The quarterback should carry the ball at about the base of his numbers with two hands. The fingers of the throwing hand need to adjust the football for throwing immediately after the snap. The quarterback's elbows must be pointed toward the

Figure 6.9

The QB uses a front-out technique and sprints out.

Figure 6.10

The QB uses a reverse pivot and rolls out.

ground and the football held close to his body. Both hands equally grip the football while it is held in the natural running position at the base of the numbers. His arms have to move fluidly back and forth during the sprint-out or rollout, much like a track sprinter's arms.

As soon as the quarterback breaks containment, he makes every effort to get squared up on target while moving toward the potential receiver. When he throws on-the-run, the quarterback's release is more out in front of his body because of momentum and body thrust. Throwing while moving requires different mechanics, so the quarterback has to engage in throwing on-the-run drills if he is to become proficient. Throwing on the run can be dramatically improved with correct technique and repetition. Some tremendous rollout or sprint-out quarterbacks have advanced this form of passing action—Fran Tarkenton, Bob Griese, and Randal Cunningham, to name three.

The best drills to foster passing while running are the follow-through position drill, straight line drill, squared-up drill, slide and throw drill, and the beat outside pass rush drill.

Follow-Through Position Drill

The quarterback stands 10 yards from another player, with his right foot forward (if right handed) so that weight distribution is primarily on the front foot. This is the follow-through position from which the quarterback passes when throwing on the run. The ball is held at the natural throwing position (about at the base of the numbers), and the football is delivered from that position.

Straight Line Drill

In the straight line drill, one quarterback runs directly at another and throws, using the pass-on-the-run technique. The quarterback must square up to the man he is passing the football to and throw off the lead foot. The distance between the two participants can vary, but about 10 yards release to catch best serves this drill. A receiver can serve as the catcher for the drill, and all the quarterbacks on the team can execute throws. The drill can be reset at the original site, or the quarterbacks can do a run by and set up behind the receiver.

Squared-Up Drill

The quarterback sets up behind the center (or from a spot if the center isn't available) and moves toward another player in the sprint-out or rollout action. Stress the adjusting action to the upfield man. The quarterback must get a squared position on the player he is throwing to and throw off his front foot.

Slide and Throw Drill

This drill is very good for improving the quarterback's view of the field and teaching him to buy time after setting up. The quarterback takes a five- or seven-step drop, then moves to one side or the other to an open lane. An inside rusher attacks the quarterback after counting to two. While in the drop, the quarterback feels the rush, sets up, and moves away from the pass rusher to the nearest lane. Two defensive linemen should be placed over imaginary offensive guards. The coach stands behind the quarterback about 10 yards from the line of scrimmage and points to which defender he wants to rush. Two large bags are placed to simulate the lanes to both sides of the quarterback. The signal caller quickly slides his feet once he recognizes the inside rush and gets squared up on the receiver. He should also step up when he slides his feet. Both hands should be on the football throughout the drill. Two receivers can be placed upfield to catch the ball.

No other drill helps a quarterback learn to deal with the outside pass rush like the beat outside pass rush drill. The quarterback holds the football to simulate taking the snap. He executes his drop (five- or seven-step), sets up, and feels a pass rush coming from the outside. On recognition of the pressure, he accelerates his setup and steps up quickly inside the rusher. This drill has two defenders lined up just outside where a tight end normally aligns. Rushers are told to rush the back-side shoulder of the quarterback and not touch his throwing arm. The coach stands behind the quarterback at about 10 yards deep, looking for his reaction and proper foot movement. Both outside defenders count to two and then attack the setup position of the quarterback, either at the five-step or seven-step foot plant of the quarterback. A receiver should be placed upfield to catch the throw.

CHAPTER 7

PASSING TECHNIQUES

While coaching at the University of Oregon in 1971, I was fortunate enough to have some very talented athletes. Among them were Pro Bowl tight end Russ Francis and quarterback Hall of Famer Dan Fouts. Francis could literally throw the football almost the length of the football field. Fouts had a good arm but could not match this feat, despite being one of the greatest quarterbacks to ever play the game. It was Fouts' mucho other assets that contributed to his success. He could throw the football when and where he wanted to with regularity. Accuracy and timing are the *basis* for productive passing. Velocity is certainly important but only as it relates to ball placement and release time.

This chapter explores all the aspects of technique involved in passing the football, as well as analyzes throwing problems and outlines applicable solutions. The quality of the throw depends on whether it progressed through the sequential process correctly or not. A clear understanding of the methodology involved when passing the ball encourages and allows for self-evaluation plus refinement of delivery. Ball release begins with proper placement of the throwing hand on the football. This is commonly referred to as the *grip*.

Gripping the Football

Gripping the football correctly affects the throwing mechanics and balance of the ball. In other chapters, grip has been discussed as it relates to other subjects. But here the process is detailed. The grip is to throwing what stance is to running. Without proper spacing of the fingers on the ball, there will be improper balance of the ball and lack of control. When fingers are placed incorrectly, the football will not leave the hand with the velocity or precision needed.

So, the question is then, what is an appropriate grip? An appropriate grip varies from one person to another. There is no specific relevant spacing or placement of the hand on the football. Size of hands and length of fingers always influence placement of the hand. Generally one to three fingers need to cross the laces to provide enough control and pressure on the surface of the ball. All fingers are used to a degree in the balance of the football, but in terms of importance to passing, the index finger is the most crucial.

During the off-season, the quarterback should determine through experimentation the best grip for him. Sometimes, it's simply a matter of adjusting the finger spread or placement of the index finger, and a better passer is born. A quarterback is quick to know by the feel if his grip is good for him.

The Thumb

To be most effective when gripping the football, a passer's throwing hand ought to cover more than 50 percent of the ball. Just where and how the football rests in the hand varies from person to person, but the common denominator is the ability to control both velocity and accuracy.

The thumb supplies the leverage and to some degree pushes the ball during the release. The position and angle of the thumb have everything to do with the amount of push and control and balance of the ball. Generally the larger the hand, the more the thumb points toward the back end of the football. A quarterback with a small hand tends to move the thumb more toward the middle of the ball. Be aware of the space between the thumb and palm and the football. Usually this space should not exceed 1/2 inch. A good way to check this space is to be sure the index finger of the nonthrowing hand can be inserted between the palm and the football (figure 7.1).

Figure 7.1

The index finger of the nonthrowing hand should fit in the space between the palm and the football.

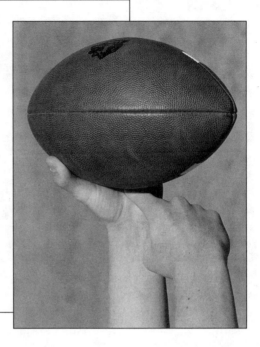

The Forefinger

You will know the forefinger is being placed correctly on the ball by noting how accurately the ball is thrown. The finger's angle should be about 45 degrees to the back point of the ball. This angle should change if the ball does not leave the grip true in its course. Like the thumb, the forefinger ought to be placed on the football in accordance with hand size so as to properly propel the ball.

The forefinger is the last finger to leave the grip on the football, promoting precise ball direction. This finger also aids in the rotation and propulsion of the ball itself.

Other Fingers

Middle, fourth, and little fingers are also of monumental importance in gripping the pigskin (figure 7.2). Ideally the middle finger is just on or just off the laces and is pointed vertically across the ball. The fourth finger should have contact with the laces, at least to the first knuckle overlapping the laces. A passer's little finger ideally needs to touch the laces and be angled slightly toward the back nose of the football.

Figure 7.2

Correct finger position on the football. The middle finger points vertically across the ball, just touching the laces; the first knuckle of the ring finger overlaps the laces; and the little finger touches the laces and is angled slightly toward the back of the ball.

Spacing

The distance between the fingers is called the *spread* and provides stability to the overall grip. A grip has to feature wide enough finger spacing to allow the quarterback to hold the ball securely in one hand while rotating his arm in a complete circle. Another way to test if the grip is appropriate is to have the quarterback hold the football with the throwing hand extended down toward the ground while running. If the ball doesn't fall out of his grip, then the grip is appropriate.

Another aspect of spacing is the distance between the football and the palm of the throwing hand. This space is critical for proper feel because the palm does not provide assistance to the delivery process other than to act to connect the fingers with the grip itself. In fact, when the football rests too close to the palm, it negatively affects the pushing of the ball on the release.

Proper Throwing Mechanics

No doubt some quarterbacks succeed even though they use unsound delivery tactics because they are gifted with physical talent and can overcome whatever unsound moves they make. Unsound delivery here refers to any position of the body or arm that reduces fluidity, velocity, or accuracy.

Body type and arm length influence the motion of delivery and differ from one quarterback to another. However, there are some general considerations that need to be incorporated into the passing process for all quarterbacks. Quarterbacks should be taught the proper mechanics so that they can find the most effective way for them to deliver the ball consistently.

Arm Path During Delivery

Chapter 8 discusses passing action and the throwing process as it relates to specific passes. Passing the football requires certain basic movements to perform a successful delivery. This chapter zeroes in on the total arm rotation movement.

A quarterback follows some fundamental steps as his arm ascends and descends through the throwing motion. These steps include arm position, shoulder position, and angle of the football, from the beginning of the throw to the final release (figure 7.3). Arm action is like a ladder with steps going up and down.

For the first step, a right-handed quarterback uses his left hand to push the ball from the number position to begin the throwing action. The left hand comes off the ball naturally at about shoulder height.

Next, the throwing-arm elbow extends out and back slightly higher than the wrist until the ball reaches shoulder level. The football is lifted up from the shoulder to a position behind and higher than the elbow. The distance from the body to the ball depends on the length of the quarterback's arm.

In step three, the football is turned outward from the body. The end of the ball away from the quarterback should be tilted slightly up.

Next, the upfield shoulder and hip must turn in sequence with the back hip and shoulder as needed for body momentum, allowing a full forward thrust of the arm to begin the throwing action.

Figure 7.3

Proper throwing sequence (right-handed QB).

(*a*) The left hand comes off the ball near the shoulder. The elbow extends out and back until the ball reaches shoulder level.

(*b*) The ball is turned out with the end slightly tilted. The upfield shoulder and hip turn in sequence with the back hip and shoulder as the throwing arm moves forward.

(c) The throwing-arm elbow leads the delivery as the front hip and shoulder open. The front foot steps as the front hip opens in the direction of the throw.

As forward delivery begins, the elbow of the throwing arm leads while the front hip and shoulder open, providing momentum and eventually full range of motion for the arm.

The football turns naturally from a pointed-out position to straight about when the ball is at its highest place in the arc of the delivery.

The direction of the throw should be in line with the quarterback's belly button when the ball leaves his hand.

The front foot steps as that hip opens in the direction the football is going to be thrown. A whipping twist of the lead or front hip must occur as this step is being taken. This rotation provides complete freedom for hip rotation as the ball is being thrown.

The elevation of the football nose varies with the type of pass being thrown, but the nose must be positioned correctly as the ball leaves the hand. Deeper passes require more nose elevation at the peak of the arm arc.

The fingers leave the ball in a little finger, fourth finger, middle finger, thumb, and index finger sequence. The index finger provides accuracy and spin to the ball.

Velocity is generated from the time the passing action begins until the football is about straight over the head. Follow-through takes over at this point and does not end until the football leaves the index finger.

After the football leaves the hand, the wrist goes from straight to turned out. This ensures that there is complete follow-through. The back is bent a little at this point, while the shoulders are square to the line of scrimmage for most throws. The elbow of the throwing arm locks up or straightens out as the football leaves the hand, providing additional push to delivery.

Contributing Aspects to Passing Mechanics

Quarterback passing fundamentals incorporate four absolutes: stance, exchange, setup, and release. Equal stress is placed on all four phases of passing, but releasing the football is the most vital. With respect to any or all of these factors, a quarterback may need some minor deviation with the total delivery process to best suit his talents.

There is no perfect way to execute these techniques but rather a basically sound procedure that applies to the uniqueness of the individual quarterback. In short, passing mechanics differ somewhat from one person to the next, but what is important is that each quarterback perfects his own attributes within the throwing process.

Use of Head and Eyes

Throwing mechanics change when the quarterback uses the turn-away/look-off method. Often the quarterback will need to reposition his upper body quickly to get the ball off. With this procedure, the football should be carried at the top of the numbers for quick release.

Defensive backs are trained to read the quarterback's body language in most forms of zone coverage. Quarterbacks can easily misdirect or influence the defensive back's position. However, it is difficult and unproductive for a quarterback to use his shoulders, head, or eyes to affect the defender when throwing shorter passes, as he must get rid of the football quickly. Being on time with the delivery far outweighs the value of faking. But in intermediate plays, such as screens, curls, and layer patterns, faking technique can be effective. Every day quarterbacks must practice looking away or turning to one side, then coming back to throw to the other side. Always use this technique when throwing crossing routes, deep curls, intermediate to deep outs, seams, post routes, flags, multiple cutting patterns, and screens. Build the desired fake into each pass pattern. The fake may be a staring look or a scanning move.

© Newsport Photography

▪ Kurt Warner uses his body language and his eyes to mislead the defense.

Adjusting Body and Feet in the Throwing Process

A lot of people do not realize how critical the quarterback's feet are in the passing process. The advice "Always throw the football with your feet under you" is basically correct, as the feet provide stability for accuracy and velocity. Like other fundamentals, game situations such as scrambling or backing away from a pass rusher sometimes do not allow the ideal to occur. Whenever possible, the quarterback should use correct foot position to encourage body balance, quick delivery, proper follow-through, and body push.

There is no perfectly correct way to manage the body, but there are some basic guidelines that help develop ideal body alignment for the quarterback. The quarterback's shoulders and hips should face the receiver as the ball leaves his throwing hand. The body is propelled when the passer's lead foot steps in the direction of the receiver. The quarterback should force his front upfield shoulder to open completely. Tell the quarterback to attempt to push his belly button in the direction of the released football as his arm begins its downward cycle in the delivery. The quarterback's weight shifts from his back foot to his front foot when passing from a stationary position to encourage follow-through.

The transfer of weight is not productive when the quarterback is running. That is why it is more difficult to throw as hard or be on target when the passer is on the move. When the quarterback passes while moving, his weight is always forward on his front foot. He throws from his follow-through position because of the progression of the weight transfer to the follow-through.

Ball Position

The only way a football can arrive on time with proper velocity and accuracy is for the football's position to be in the appropriate spot before the throwing action begins. The ball should be placed between the numbers and the shoulder, depending on how soon the ball is to be thrown and the quarterback's physical makeup.

The higher the football is held, the faster the ball can get away if a hitch isn't used or the ball isn't lowered before the upward movement of the delivery begins. Some pass patterns, however, require specific placement of the football in the prerelease stage; for example, in quick set passes, the ball must be held higher than normal.

For most passes, ideal ball position is about at the top of the numbers. The ball is gripped four to six inches away from the body. It is advantageous to begin delivery from this position. The arc of delivery and full range of motion are important, encouraging a tight spiral with zip on the pigskin whenever possible.

Finding a Lane

To be an effective passer, the quarterback must use his peripheral vision to locate seams in the pass rush through which to throw the football. These lanes are always present, so it's just a matter of the quarterback simply sliding his feet in the best lane. Quarterbacks who lack height must perfect this method if they are to be successful. Mastering this task takes realistic practice against an aggressive pass rush.

A quarterback soon learns to find lanes in different places when working against a three-, four-, or five-man rush. The maneuvering itself, however, is natural and instinctive and thus should not be a programmed or predetermined move. Lanes not only provide for improved vision but also allow the signal caller to step up and throw the football. Stepping up places outside rushers behind the quarterback's throwing track, providing still another aspect of passing in a lane.

Man rather than zone protection is more conducive to the formation of lanes. Nonetheless, there are always openings to slide to, and the quarterback's job is to be aware of these throwing positions. It should also be noted that if zone protection is used lanes are less needed, as the nature of zone protection is firmer and confronts the pass rusher closer to the line of scrimmage. Because of the increased space between the quarterback and rushers, throwing lanes are not as necessary.

Following a Quarterback's Instincts

During a game at the University of Oregon in 1970, against our rival Oregon State, Dan Fouts wanted to open the game with a streak or go route down the sideline. As his position coach, I had another idea but let Dan have his way. The result was a 60-yard completion! Often the quarterback has a feel for what to do or what not to do. Good coaching is to go with the quarterback's instincts as much as possible, within reason. By the way, it was raining so hard it was nearly impossible to even see 60 yards! Dan's coordination of feet and arm working together provided the timing for the play; anticipation replaced vision.

Feet and Arm Working Together

I can't emphasize enough the importance of the feet and arm working together. Accuracy and velocity are affected positively or negatively by the coordination of a quarterback's feet and arm. If the feet are ahead of the arm in the throwing process, the ball dives or sails. When the arm is ahead of the feet, the ball lacks velocity.

Whenever possible a quarterback should step in the direction he is intending to pass to ensure both accuracy and velocity. The throwing arm needs to be at about the middle of the arm arc when the lead foot strikes the ground. This position should place the football at the end of the momentum phase of the throwing release.

It is more difficult for a right-handed quarterback to pass the football to his left than it is to his right, particularly when the throw to the left is a quick one. The quarterback can use one of two techniques to address this challenge: the back-out/backpedal method or the approach where the hip opens to the left. The backpedal procedure provides better vision and allows the arm to come through quickly when the hips are square to the line of scrimmage. The quarterback drops back after receiving the exchange, with short sliding steps, keeping his shoulders square to the line of scrimmage, his weight back, and the ball gripped in both hands.

In the open-hip approach, the quarterback's final step of his drop lands in a 45-degree angle to the line of scrimmage (figure 7.4). This allows his arm to come through faster because the front hip is open to the left. The open hip and lead shoulder are forced open when the back foot is set to the right of the drop lane line.

Figure 7.4

The open-hip method used by a right-handed QB to throw to the left.

A right-handed quarterback who is throwing to the left while on the run tends to be erratic because his body is so far ahead of his arm. There is little chance for velocity or follow-through. The solution is to do one of two things: either turn the body around and go upfield so that the throwing arm is closer to the body or slow the running gait during the delivery.

There are many things that assist a quarterback's performance, but nothing can compare with good, old basic fundamentals. When a quarterback adheres to sound fundamentals, he increases his ability to throw the football—period. Yes, it's the little things that comprise the basics and make the difference in what is recorded on the scoreboard at the end of each contest. In short, a quarterback who does his job the right way uses his passing skills to the fullest. Good passers get better when they accept and apply correct mechanics.

Any and every quarterback can improve regardless of his present effectiveness. All skills can be vastly improved with more reps and refinement—that's a fact. There are no shortcuts to perfection, especially so when it comes to throwing the football.

There are four common throwing situations that trouble a quarterback at one time or another. To recognize these difficulties and deal with them is imperative to the consistency of a passer. Once a quarterback determines he is having difficulty with his mechanics, it's a matter of correction, knowing what to do and doing it.

Arm Not Strong Enough

It is rough on a quarterback when his arm is not strong enough, but there are two approaches to the solution.

First, try changing the delivery steps of the quarterback to allow more body and momentum into the pass. Set the quarterback a little deeper than normal (one to two steps). From this position, he must use a crossover/slide approach to shuffle to the delivery. Setting up deeper encourages stepping up quickly, with room, allowing the body action to get ahead of the arm and forcing the upper body, including the arm, to catch up. If the quarterback is right handed, he needs to set his back foot, then drive this same foot with a large overlapping step so as to step over his lead foot. He must keep his body low in the beginning, with his knees bent, well until push off from the back leg begins. The left foot then takes a slide step, about the distance necessary to place the quarterback in a natural throwing position, generally about a foot wider than shoulder width. Remember that distance will vary with leg length. Be sure the back shoulder is down and the back knee is bent until delivery begins. Be sure the player opens up his hip and chest to allow complete body follow-through, allowing full arm rotation. The end result adds additional momentum to the throw.

Another way to improve a weak arm or put more zest into a quarterback's throw is to use arm strengthening drills. These drills improve arm strength by removing the body momentum from the throw. Before starting any of these drills, the quarterback should warm up his arm to prevent it from getting sore.

All four of the throwing drills are hard on the arm, particularly if used extensively, and should not be overdone. If a sore arm occurs, ease up by taking fewer repetitions. Mix these drills with ones that encourage follow-through so that stress is placed on the body instead of the arm. Use arm strengthening drills no more than half of the throwing workout time. These drills should be the focus of off-season work; during the season, form passing should primarily be used. To help the strengthening process, use a weighted ball (only for off-season training).

Squeezing a small ball in the palm of the throwing hand can also enhance arm strength. Using a five-pound dumbbell to simulate the throwing action can also help.

Throws From Knees

The quarterback kneels on both knees and throws to a receiver about 10 yards away (approximately 20 throws). Every day the quarterback increases the length of his throw until he can no longer throw the ball in a straight line. When this happens, he stays at this distance for a few days, then progresses farther, at the rate of one yard per day to a distance of 10 additional yards. Demand proper grip and two hands on the football until the supporting hand (the left, if right handed) naturally comes off the ball in the throwing action. Continue to work at this distance until the quarterback shows improvement in his arm strength. This drill can be done in the off-season.

Wrong Foot Forward

This throwing drill also will help strengthen the arm. If right handed, the quarterback places his right foot slightly ahead of his left and stands with a wide enough base to have good balance. He throws to a receiver using the same progression as the two-knee drill. Stress proper grip, body balance, and follow-through. The quarterback should not step forward and must keep his weight on his right foot. Ideally, the quarterback would concentrate on this drill for three to four minutes or 20 repetitions.

Feet Together

The quarterback stands with his feet together and parallel, about shoulder width apart. He throws the ball to a receiver. Again, 20 repetitions is the desired goal, at a distance of about 10 yards. The quarterback's feet should remain still; he does not step into the throw. The progression is the same as for other drills. His body weight is balanced on both feet. This drill develops upper-body mechanics and velocity.

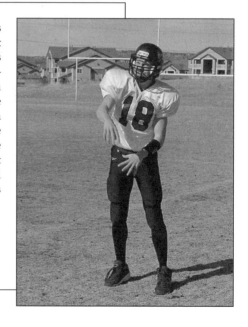

Throw Stepping Backward

In this drill, the quarterback steps backward with his right foot (if he's right handed) as he throws the ball. As is the case in all throwing drills, about three to four minutes or 20 throws are appropriate. The progression is the same as for the other drills. Follow-through is interrupted in this drill, and there is less accuracy with the throw. Start at 10 yards from the receiver and progress from there.

Ball Wobbles

Two common errors may cause the football to wobble. First, the wrist may not be straight when the ball is projected forward in the throwing motion. If the quarterback's throwing wrist is turned out when his little finger comes off the football, the ball will not sail true from the hand, causing the front nose to move laterally. The solution is to make sure the wrist stays straight, parallel to the body, with the fingers directly upward, until the arm begins its downward movement during the delivery. At that time, the fingers come off the football naturally, starting with the little finger.

The second common cause of ball wobble is improper spacing of the fingers. A passer's hand ideally should cover more than 50 percent of the football, and no more than three fingers should cover the laces. When more than three fingers cross the laces or the hand doesn't cover more than 50 percent of the ball, the fingers are not spread enough. When the fingers are too close together (even if hand size is the reason), there is not good ball control. The result is wobble caused by the quarterback's lack of balance while gripping the football. A comfortable grip to control the football is critical for throwing a tight spiral. Concentration on ball wobble can be stressed in all throwing drills.

Nosing the Ball Into the Ground

Nosing the ball is the most frequent error. There are three major causes. The first cause is incorrect ball position in the throwing hand. The space between the palm of the hand and the ball must allow the ball to leave the hand at the correct projection. By adjusting the space—and there must be space—you can add lift to the football or put the ball on a downward trajectory.

Second, passers who one hand the ball often throw it without follow-through, which pushes the pigskin in a downward sailing trajectory. The lead hand under or on the side of the ball should be maintained until just before forward arm action begins. Keep the left hand on the ball to secure it, and place the ball in the correct natural delivery position, which helps with follow-through.

Third, poor follow-through technique influences the nose of the football. Quarterbacks who open the front hip up too soon, too much, or take too big a throwing step regularly throw the ball into the ground. Follow-through begins too rapidly. The solution is to change follow-through so that the front shoulder does not drop or pull away too much or too rapidly from the throwing arm. The lead shoulder and throwing arm work in concert with each other. Playing catch using the appropriate steps for follow-through is the best way to correct this problem.

Nose of Ball Too Flat

Not getting lift on the football can be caused by not using the left hand to load or cock the throwing arm. For a right-handed passer, when the left hand is not kept on the football slightly under and to the side, the ball does not get into the appropriate position to leave the throwing hand, with the nose elevated. Because all deeper passes and touch throws depend on nose elevation, this is a critical fundamental to learn.

The quarterback who does not get his back shoulder down on his final step of the drop or setup causes the nose of the ball to remain flat. On the release, the shoulder must come up, but it's the transfer of weight and lift from the back leg, hip, and shoulder to the front leg and hip that allows speed and elevation on the ball.

The back knee, bending to a straight position, is similar to a player accelerating forward and upward out of his stance. The action is much like a baseball hitter stepping into a pitch to hit. The center of gravity must shift from the back leg, through the center of the body, to the front leg. Correct weight transfer and shoulder-level change are most important to the delivery. Like dealing with the problem of the nose being down, correcting this flaw can be done by correcting footwork while the quarterback is playing catch.

CHAPTER 8

TYPES OF PASSES

The word "essential" best describes the content of this chapter. Understanding this material and applying the details are vital to understanding what it takes to be an effective passer. The basic fundamentals in the art of passing are directly tied to a quarterback's success. Degree of excellence is also linked to the conquest of running two distinct types of pass plays.

A requirement for all quarterbacks is to understand, and hopefully master, the rudimentary aspects of both the rhythm and discipline of passing. These two facets are incorporated into each and every pass thrown. The effectiveness of any signal caller evolves from whatever skill he demonstrates in these two elements of pass plays.

This chapter takes a hard look at rhythm and discipline passing. But before an examination of these two specific forms of pass offense is presented, some of the factors that contribute to successfully throwing the football within the framework of these categories will be explored. All of these components of passing can be categorized as either physical or mental elements but overlap somewhat.

Givens for a productive passer are an adequate arm, above-average foot movement, good work habits, a competitive attitude, some degree of mental toughness, and basic football intelligence. With these attributes, a signal caller will have some success throwing the football. Add to this mix sound fundamentals, and a quarterback can dominate the game.

A quarterback with these assets is well on his way to becoming a prolific passer. His awareness of environmental factors also has a great impact on his ability to throw the ball. Add to this his understanding of the many aspects of passing, and it will lift him to even more success. For a signal caller, performance in the passing game is linked to his knowledge and commitment to properly use all of his mental and physical tools.

Learning in the Game

While working at Portland State, I had the privilege to tutor one of the truly outstanding pinpoint college passers of his time, Tim Von Dulm. Tim, who established many passing records for the Vikings, had a special gift of getting the football to the correct place at the right time. He was a master at visualizing play execution before the ball was snapped into his hands.

One cold Saturday, Tim was having good success against Idaho State, but he threw a costly interception, which made him mad—not at anyone except himself. His explanation was that he didn't anticipate correctly. Later, as I studied the videotape, I determined that he was not wrong on his decision. Tim not only perceived each play during each game, he self-evaluated them. This young man learned from his successful plays, as well as his misfires. His performance always incorporated insightfulness, pregame study, established habits, and confidence. It is no wonder he set an NCAA record while at Portland State for consecutive completions without an interception.

Precision Passing

Precision passing and anticipating is a learned art. It can be developed and perfected. Most great quarterbacks have this asset and use it to the max. Dan Fouts had it, Norv Turner had it, Dave Dickenson had it, as did Tim Von Dulm. All were extremely successful at throwing the football, and a big part of the reason was their effectiveness in ball placement and timing.

There are few phases of quarterback technique more important than getting rid of the football quickly. Not enough quarterbacks demonstrate this asset. Mastering quick release can be accomplished only by high-speed repetition of the field general's release process. Improvement starts with proper ball position.

In general, the higher the ball is held when the throwing process begins, the quicker the release. Approximately the top of the numbers is the place from which to propel the ball for quick passes (figure 8.1). Ball position can be altered higher or lower, depending on body type and arm length.

Figure 8.1

Holding the football at the top of the numbers.

When the quarterback lowers the football from the beginning point (hitch) of the throwing action, he starts the delivery at too high a point. If the ball leaves the throwing hand too late, it needs to be raised higher to begin the throwing action.

A coach can help the overall procedure by standing behind the quarterback during drills and shouting, "Get rid of it!" to stress a quicker release. This emphasizes the importance of the quick release. In this way, the quarterback is conditioned to anticipate firing the football more rapidly, learning to prioritize this phase of the throwing process. Another method is to use a stopwatch to time every throw the quarterback makes in drills to judge whether the release time is fast enough.

Teach the quarterback in drills to have the ball on its way before the receiver is in position to catch it. On short routes in which the quarterback takes a three-step drop or fewer steps, he should let the ball go one receiver step before the receiver gets to the designated field position or to the anticipated spot of reception. This mega-speed passing is almost impossible to defend effectively. When the quarterback is in a five-step drop, he anticipates the receiver's reception point about two steps before the catch point. On a seven-step drop, he uses a three-step anticipation, depending on the type of route the receiver runs.

This concept applies even when the quarterback is throwing the ball on the run, such as in rollout, play action, or sprint-out passes. In fact, because it's more difficult to get enough umph on the football when on the run, the quarterback may need an even earlier anticipation. Use videotape of practice sessions with the quarterback so that he can see himself executing this procedure over and over. This will ensure that he understands how to time his throws. Anticipation passing is customized to each signal caller, so any quarterback can perfect this skill.

Handling Pressure

The ability to deal with an overwhelming defensive pass rush is a vital area of quarterbacking. A quarterback can improve this skill through recognition of the opponent's attack strategy and by handling the overload situation a defense might use. School the quarterback on presnap alignment reads and potential rush. Use a blackboard, walk-throughs, and teaching videotapes (cutups) to train him to identify likely pressure before the ball comes up.

The key is that the signal caller must know how many blockers he has available at all times and on each play to match the number of likely rushers. When the number of rushers exceeds that of offensive blockers, the quarterback is responsible for defeating this defensive scheme by getting rid of the ball quickly or changing the play to allow for necessary protection.

Another, more effective procedure is to control the opposition's pass rush. Penalize the defense for their pressure tactics with presnap play selection that is carefully thought out long before the quarterback gets on the firing line. There is no better way to dismantle defensive force than to beat it with a nondefendable play. Screen pass; short, quick route; sweep away from pressure side; quick-hitting straight ahead

© The Sporting Image/Kirby Lee

■ To beat a swarming pass rush, Jeff Garcia gets rid of the ball quickly.

plays; pass from shotgun formation; or site adjustment communication are among the ways to punish a defense for their aggressive tactics. Any or all of these will require committed practice time to not only ensure neutralization but to create retribution.

Examples of penalizing pressure are dumping the ball to a back to beat an outside linebacker blitz (figure 8.2a) or dumping the ball to the tight end versus an inside linebacker blitz (figure 8.2b).

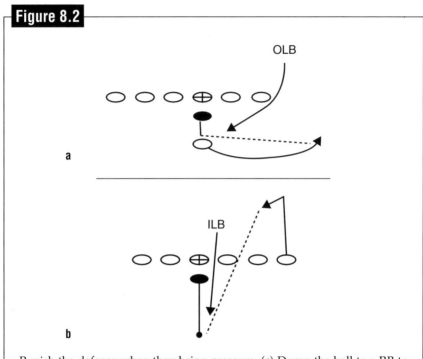

Figure 8.2

Punish the defense when they bring pressure. (*a*) Dump the ball to a RB to beat an outside blitz. (*b*) Dump the ball to a TE to beat an inside LB rush.

Rhythm and Timing Passes

Let's now explore the most common classification of throwing the football. This type of throwing is called *rhythm passing*. Some quarterbacks are pretty good at throwing the football to the right place at the correct time. Too few though are really excellent at this skill. It takes good hand, eye, and foot coordination. Rhythm throws are predetermined pass plays in which the receiver is at a specific place when the quarterback's back foot sets and the ball is off. These types of passes include outs, fakes, slants, and swings. Practicing rhythm throwing over and over is the best way to perfect this art.

Working with a receiver is important if a quarterback is to refine this type of pass. What makes the pass successful is the timing of the relationship between the quarterback and the receiver. This means matching the quarterback drop level with the receiver cut, break, or stop point. Three-step drops hook up with specific routes, as do five- or seven-step setups.

Rhythm passes involve anticipation of where the receiver will be. Most of the time, the receiver will not even reach the designated place when the football leaves the field general's hand. With the exception of fades or swing throws, rhythm passes are always propelled with maximum zip on the ball.

Trajectory of a rhythm pass is likewise most important. When the quarterback throws rhythm passes to a spot, the placement of the pass is crucial. Out routes need to be thrown low and to the sideline. Hitch passes should hit the receiver's numbers. Slants must be thrown waist high. Fades against the sideline should be thrown over the inside shoulder of the receiver. Correct placement allows for the easiest catch possible, keeping the ball away from the defender and ensuring the least opponent contact or impact on the receiver.

Rhythm passes are high-percentage completion throws because the quarterback and receiver work on timing, while the defender has to react. The receiver's break and the quarterback's throw are precise. This style of passing can be worked on year-round. One receiver and a quarterback can acquire mucho reps at desired routes, fine-tuning each route. A second or multiple receivers are not needed to perfect rhythm passes.

Disciplined Passing

Disciplined throws are passes that require reads or keying. Disciplined passing plays involve sophistication and complexity. When and where the quarterback throws the football depend on the defensive coverage, specifically the coverage the opponent implements and how they play it. This tells the quarterback who will be open. Because each coverage uses given strengths and weaknesses, the purpose of discipline passing is to exploit the defense's weaknesses and evade their strengths.

Attacking a coverage, which is the crux of discipline passing, requires putting two or more receivers in a pattern (see figures 8.3, 8.4, and 8.5). One or more receivers act as decoys and try to influence a portion of the coverage, permitting another receiver to get open. This can be done with up to four receivers, with two or three receivers running outs at different levels and the quarterback throwing to the open man. Receivers also can be put in layers across the middle of the field. Another discipline passing approach is to run curls at different levels. Depending on coverage, the quarterback throws to the open player according to the undercover drops.

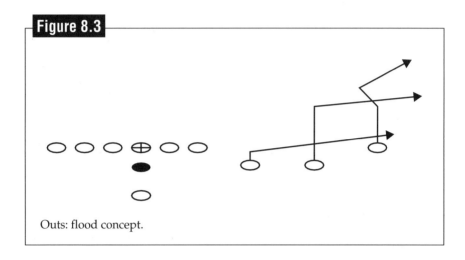

Figure 8.3

Outs: flood concept.

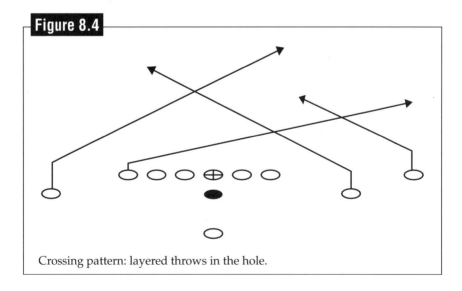

Figure 8.4

Crossing pattern: layered throws in the hole.

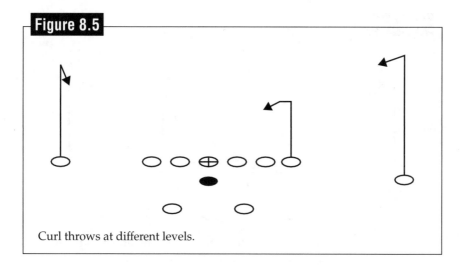

Figure 8.5

Curl throws at different levels.

Combination out patterns allow the quarterback to key the corner and throw where he isn't. A layer pattern is a read technique for the quarterback (figure 8.6). He looks for holes in the coverage as his receivers cross. The multiple curl puts two or three receivers in curl routes at different levels (figure 8.7). The quarterback keys short to keep in progression, depending on the angle and position of the linebacker drops.

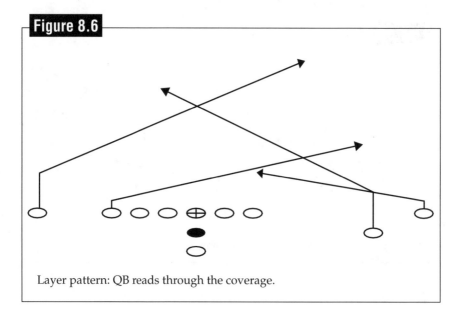

Figure 8.6

Layer pattern: QB reads through the coverage.

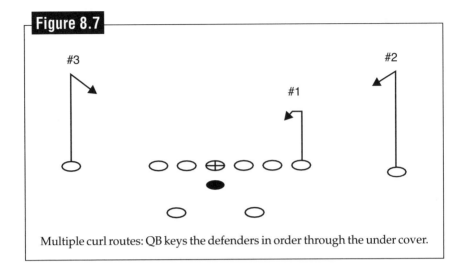

Multiple curl routes: QB keys the defenders in order through the under cover.

Keying on the three-man out pattern involves focusing on the corner only (figure 8.8). When using curl combos, the quarterback concentrates on the first linebacker inside the tight end's curl. Then he throws to the tight end if he is open. If the linebacker is in the throwing lane, the quarterback works out to the next key in the secondary. In curl combos, the next key is the outside backer or strong safety if the initial key is an inside backer.

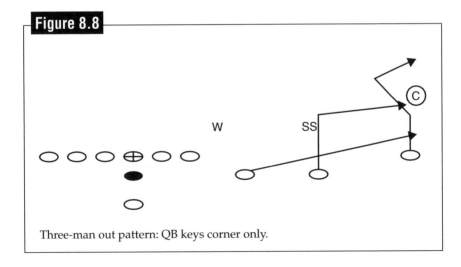

Three-man out pattern: QB keys corner only.

The Passing Tree

The life blood of any pass offense is the potency of its passing tree. A tree's pass route branches serve as the foundation for individual routes, as well as all pass patterns. Routes identified on the tree normally are the most frequently traveled or needed with the passing attack.

A passing tree trunk can be compared to a modern freeway, in that it serves as the main path for all route beginnings. The trunk, sometimes called the stem, provides the place from which specific routes exit to a predetermined site. Trunk structures provide a breaking point common to other routes, creating an illusion as to which direction a receiver will travel.

Each route on a passing tree is distinct and has its own characteristics. Most football teams identify tree routes by number but often also with names for communication purposes. So, a typical passing tree has names, as well as numbers, to describe each specific route. For example, a slant or look-in pass by name often draws the number 1 on the tree. A sideline or quick out route might have the number 2 on the tree. The number 3 on a tree is commonly a side route that puts the receiver on an out move, then on an in move. Like the 2 route, the 4 is an out but at a deeper level. Five on a tree means curl; 6, deeper out; 7, hook; 8, flag; 9, post; and zero tells the receiver to streak.

The numbers on the tree progress from lower to higher. Lower numbers reflect shorter routes, while higher ones indicate deeper plays. Odd-numbered routes break inward; even numbers cut to the outside.

Let's now examine an ideal passing tree design or makeup. There are 10 ways a receiver can go when using the tree, shown in figure 8.9. The tree is made up of the 10 fundamental routes needed in any pass offense. By no means, however, should you accept that there are only 10 essential routes in any passing scheme. The 10 routes presented here reflect what is most commonly believed to be the best-suited and proved routes.

The tree should be modified to exploit the ability of the signal caller (figure 8.10). Some quarterbacks are more capable in throwing harder, longer, softer, or quicker. For example, a slant, or 1 route, could be changed to a hitch on the tree. An 8 or 9 route also might be a read or stop route for a given quarterback.

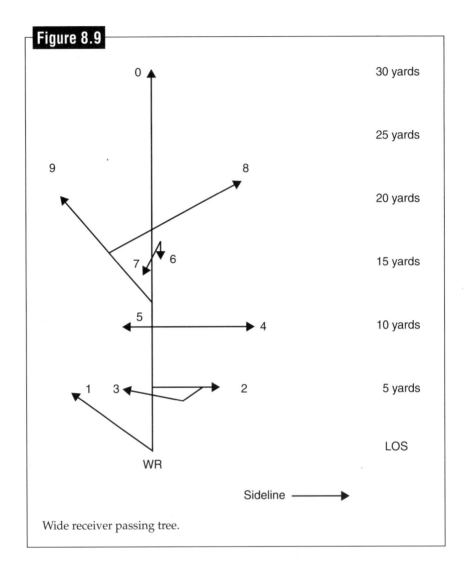

Wide receiver passing tree.

Other variations are to tailor the tree to the field general and coverage, such as adding an up route on a slant or out, calling it 1 up or 2 up. Another good addition to the tree would be 1 out or 5 go. These variations give the quarterback more options not only to complement his uniqueness but to take advantage of a particular coverage or defender.

A quarterback with the insight into the potential of each route on the tree is well on his way to being an effective passer, especially if he understands his own capability of throwing given routes and knows how to take advantage of a secondary with these plays. Each

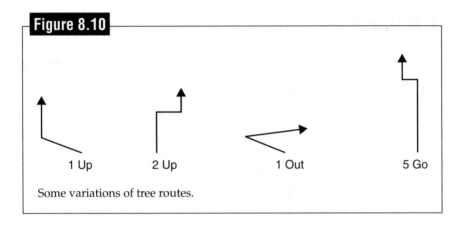

Figure 8.10

1 Up   2 Up   1 Out   5 Go

Some variations of tree routes.

route on a tree has its own intricacies. Knowing the specifics of individual routes accelerates the productivity percentage of that play. Throwing on time and anticipating the receiver and defender positions become big for the quarterback when using tree routes.

A quarterback's role in throwing each tree route can be perfected immensely through hard work. The quarterback's steps in his drop should be adjusted to each route and to specific receivers to allow for consistent success. Every route is examined from the quarterback's point of view to incorporate his footwork, mechanics, and rationale of the throw.

Like stance is to blocking, the passing tree is the heartbeat of a pass offense. This is where pass offense begins and, for some, ends. Mastery and perfection of technique involved with each route on the tree result in the quarterback taking his passing attack to the next level. It's as simple as that, and it's as easy as that.

The tree discussed to this point is for an outside receiver. Inside receivers such as the slotback, wing, tight end, or running back also use tree routes, but the routes are modified. Tree number, depth, and intent are the same for a split end or flanker as they are for an inside receiver. The difference is in the cuts. Most of the time, an inside receiver should use rounded corners or speed cuts, rather than a regular, sharp-angled cut. Rounded corners move the inside receiver to the expected landmark faster. For example, a tight end running a 2 route on the tree does not need to push upfield for five yards before cutting as a wide receiver does, but he still needs to get to the five-yard level after rounding the corner. This means when running a 2 route, he starts the outside move (speed cut) about four yards from the line of scrimmage. On the tree, shown in figure 8.11,

Figure 8.11

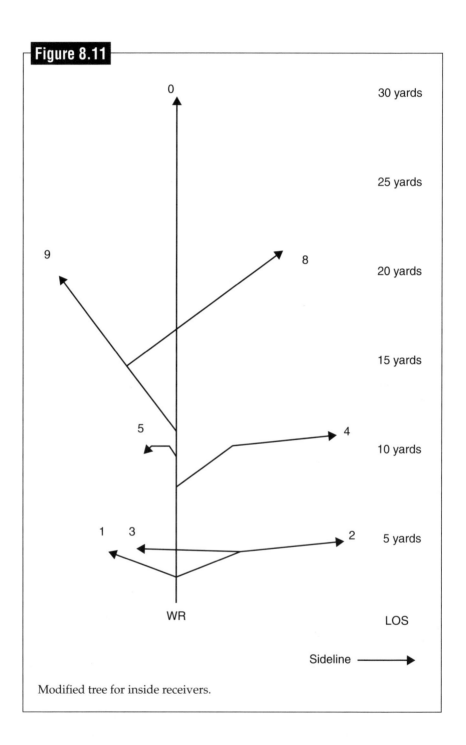

Modified tree for inside receivers.

the inside receivers do not have a 7 or 8 route because these routes normally are not highly productive ones for the inside pass catchers. However, in given situations, a 7 or 8 route can be integrated to match that situation.

Let's now examine each route for purpose and technique. Each route offers something the other ones do not. The quarterback's mechanics, timing, and anticipation differ with the specific play called. The key to mastering each route is the quarterback's understanding the receiver's moves, anticipating the throw and ball placement.

Route 1

Route—The receiver's split should not be excessively wide or short, depending on the room available. The receiver uses a quick slant versus soft cover but uses a push technique if the corner is rolled up or shaded inside. The receiver drives three steps upfield before slanting inside when he uses the drive technique. The receiver's upfield hand is held about shoulder level once the football is on the way.

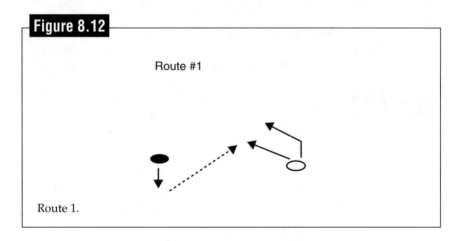

Figure 8.12

Route #1

Route 1.

Quarterback technique—The quarterback brings the football to the top of his numbers immediately after he receives the snap. He uses a quick drop and throws the ball quickly if the receiver is open. He waits until the undercover defender is not in the throwing lane if the receiver is not immediately open. This is not a step-up throw; rather, the quarterback's knees are locked, and he is flat-footed when he throws. A good follow-through ensures the tight spiral needed. The quarterback should keep the throw waist high and not above the numbers. The football must be thrown extremely hard in front of the receiver. If throwing to the left, a right-handed quarterback needs to back out of the exchange or open left immediately. When the football leaves his hand, the quarterback's depth from the original line of scrimmage is about one yard.

Coaching points—The quarterback must predetermine the side and which receiver he is going to throw to. The offensive line is aggressive with their blocking, as there must not be any defensive penetration. This route calls for minimal line splits, not exceeding two feet, and is a great automatic or sight adjustment play. It can be used anywhere on the field and against all forms of coverage. It is a good play versus the blitz and most successful when called on first down, second down, or third and normal.

Route 2

Route—The wide receiver's split should not be closer than nine yards from the sideline. Good arm pumps and leg action help sell the defense that the receiver is going deeper. The receiver can use a speed cut if the defender is playing soft. On his cut, the receiver must get his head around quickly and upfield arm to shoulder level on the break.

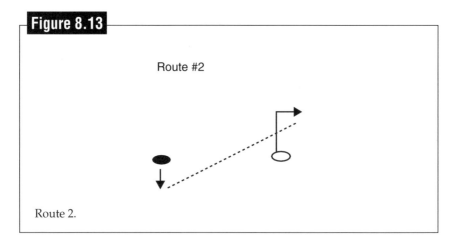

Figure 8.13

Route #2

Route 2.

Quarterback technique—The quarterback sets up with the ball at the base of the numbers. He takes five adjustable steps (short or big) in his drop. The quarterback must get the ball on the way at the breaking point of the receiver. For ideal timing, his arm motion begins as his back foot (in a five-step drop) hits the ground. The ball is thrown waist to knee high against the sideline with maximum zip. The quarterback should step in the direction of his throw and execute good follow-through. When throwing left, the quarterback uses the open-hip technique described in chapter 6. This is a rhythm pass and depends on timing for best productivity.

Coaching points—The quarterback can choose to throw to either wide receiver but must make the decision at presnap or no later than on the first two steps of his drop. This is not a good route versus man trail cover or a roll-up corner. It also is not a good route to either rollout or bootleg against because there is only a limited amount of room for the receiver to run his route and the action of both of these pass plays takes a long time to develop. Therefore, the receiver will run out of room to run his route. As a high-percentage play, this is an excellent first-down call. It is a good route to auto to or use as a sight adjustment play. Offensive linemen must block semi-aggressively to prevent defensive penetration. The offensive line must maintain good football position—knees bent, buttocks down.

Route 3

Route—The wide receiver's split should be like a 2 route split, not closer than nine yards from the sideline. This route complements 2. It is designed to get undercover, so it is best versus any form of zone cover. The receiver should use an upfield foot plant off his second step to cut back or under. The receiver must sell the 2 route to the defense with his body action.

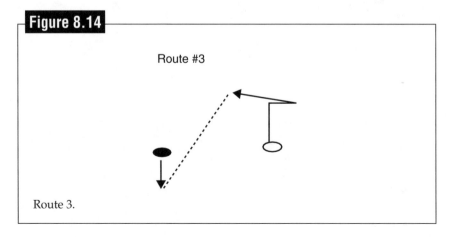

Figure 8.14

Route #3

Route 3.

Quarterback technique—Because the route takes about three seconds to develop, the quarterback has to allow the linebackers or strong safety to get their maximum drops before he throws the ball. A good extended five-step drop helps quarterback–receiver timing. The ball position is at the base of the numbers in the drop. The quarterback looks at the middle third of the field in his drop and picks up the nearest under cover on his fifth step. He steps in the direction of his pass and throws the ball hard, making sure there is no undercover man in the throwing lane. The ball has to be thrown hard between the undercover people in the hole. If this play is used versus man cover, the quarterback throws near the cutback break.

Coaching points—This route was created to beat zone coverage but is an excellent play on the goal line versus man cover. The quarterback must not lock in visually on the receiver, which telegraphs the play to the defense. When the 3 route is combined with an inside receiver clearing, it's even better. The 3 route also can be used with an inside receiver but is generally more effective when the inside receiver clears and the outside receiver runs the 3 route under the clearing.

Route 4

Route—The 4 route is an intermediate route that demands disciplined execution. The outside receiver should not use a speed cut because the football is in the air too long. The receiver should sell going deep, as if in a zero route. The wide receiver's split should not be closer than nine yards from the sideline. Inside receivers can use a speed cut on this route if coverage is soft.

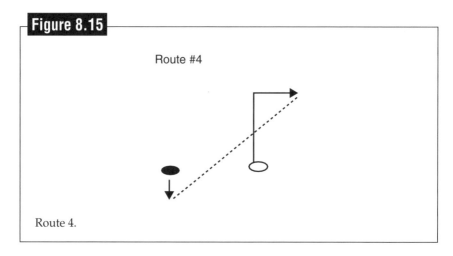

Figure 8.15

Route #4

Route 4.

Quarterback technique—The quarterback takes an extended five-step drop for a maximum depth of seven to eight yards. He carries the ball number high during his drop. The football should be thrown low and to the outside. The more velocity on the pass, the better. It's important that he get a good push off of his back setup foot and follows through. If possible, the quarterback should step up and gather momentum. While in the drop, the quarterback keys the corner but directs the secondary deep with a look-off fake. The quarterback opens his lead hip to the fullest extent to help accuracy, follow-through, and timing.

Coaching points—Do not run this route versus man trail or roll-up corner cover. The 4 route is an outstanding play, with the quarterback using sprint- or roll-out action. Be careful when throwing into the wide side of the field from a drop-back setup. This route is particularly good when a second receiver runs a route against the sideline to influence the corner, such as an 8 route or another 4 route. This is not a good route versus the blitz, and use caution when running it as a sight adjustment play.

Route 5

Route—The receiver runs a 10-yard stem, plants his outside foot, drops his buttocks, wheels around to face the quarterback, and looks for the ball. If the football is not thrown, the receiver slides to the inside, staying square to the line of scrimmage. He settles in the first hole to the inside, maintaining a knees-bent football position. The receiver's hands open, with thumbs turned inside, to provide a target number high.

Figure 8.16

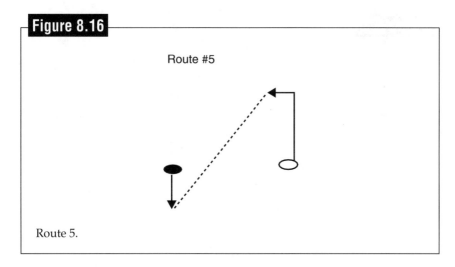

Route #5

Route 5.

Quarterback technique—The quarterback takes a maximum five-step drop (seven to eight yards). He must not rush the throw or force the football through undercover. He must wait for the receiver to find a hole between the linebackers. The quarterback's primary key is to the first inside undercover man, usually a linebacker. The quarterback influences the undercover defense with his head and eyes away from the curl zone. He steps up into the throw and places the ball chest high. If a lane is open as he plants his foot and the receiver is squared up, the quarterback throws. If a defender is in the throwing lane, the quarterback must wait until the receiver settles inside. Then he throws the ball with maximum velocity.

Coaching points—Route 5 is not as good a play when the quarterback has to throw on the run, but it is effective against any two- or three-linebacker system. The quarterback must not look at the receiver but rather keys the one inside backer nearest the curl or reads the bigger picture. This play is better versus zone cover because holes are generated naturally in undercover. The play can develop slowly, so it may not be as productive against blitzing linebackers, depending on the type of protection being used.

Route 6

Route—The receiver runs what looks like a zero route until he breaks. He makes a good inside foot plant and pushes off, coming slightly back to the line of scrimmage toward the sideline. His running-arm action while executing the stem of the route helps sell the route as zero.

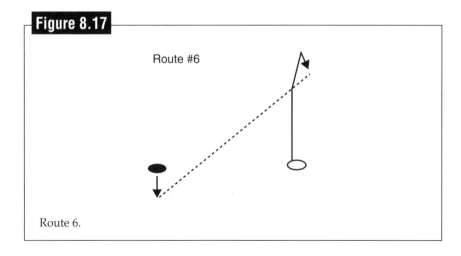

Figure 8.17

Route #6

Route 6.

Quarterback technique—In the drop, the quarterback false keys the secondary, with his head and eyes pointed to the middle one-third of the field. The quarterback drop is critical, as he needs maximum distance from the line of scrimmage (eight yards is ideal). The football must be thrown on the break of the receiver. He must throw the ball low (knee high) and to the sideline, bringing the receiver back and to the sideline. The football must be delivered with full velocity. Stepping up with a slide step allows correct weight transfer and follow-through. In the drop, the football is carried at the numbers until the quarterback's back foot sets. A good offhand lead and pull of the front shoulder ensure fluid delivery. The throwing shoulder must roll over and the wrist turn away from the body as the ball leaves the hand. The index finger helps with accuracy, as long as it is the last finger to touch the ball.

Coaching points—This is an excellent play into the short side of the field and can be most effective when there is no chance of double coverage. Setting the formation strength away from the route almost guarantees this. The play is best served with total protection employed, meaning eight guys blocking. Mirroring this route to both sides of the formation gives the quarterback the option of throwing either left or right, depending on how the corner aligns in coverage.

Route 7

Route—The stem of the 7 route should look like a 6 or zero path until the cutback spot. The receiver plants his outside foot and uses it to push off for the comeback. Going into the breaking point, the receiver must drop his buttocks and widen his feet to help slow his body momentum.

Quarterback technique—In the drop, the quarterback false keys the defenders by concentrating his head and eyes on the center of the field. Like the 6 route, the quarterback's drop is critical for the timing of the play. Five large steps or seven shorter ones work best with the 7 route. As the receiver plants his outside foot, the quarterback must have the ball on its way if the lane is open. If a defender is in front of the receiver, the quarterback holds up on the throw and lets the receiver come back toward the line of scrimmage. The football is thrown as hard as possible about waist high. Stepping up, as well as pointing the lead foot in the direction of the pass, provides necessary momentum and follow-through. The quarterback's belly

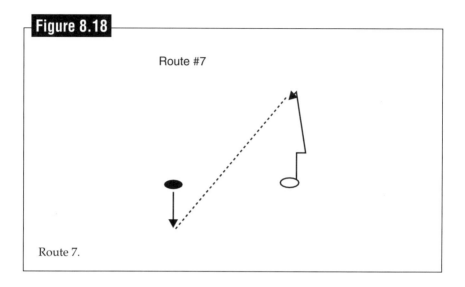

Figure 8.18

Route #7

Route 7.

button is pointed directly at the receiver as the ball leaves his hand and his front hip opens.

Coaching points—The quarterback keys the lane by focusing on the defender located to the inside of the receiver as the route break begins. Usually the defender is a linebacker but can be a strong safety or even a corner in some coverages. The 7 route normally is not a good one for inside receivers, although it can be used against some forms of man or soft zone coverage.

An inside receiver running a 5 route complements well an outside receiver executing a 7, as the quarterback can visually see both routes developing at the same time.

Route 8

Route—The complexity of this route is obvious, yet it meshes well with the post route 9. Double-cut moves, as with the 8 route, often deepen or turn the free safety. The move off the stem looks like a post route until the receiver cuts to the flag. In the flag part of the route, the receiver reads and decides whether to go to the flag or break off, depending on whether the defender plays the route under or over.

Quarterback technique—The quarterback must take a maximum drop (eight yards). He should pump fake the post route. The football is thrown with arc and to the outside shoulder of the receiver. Good

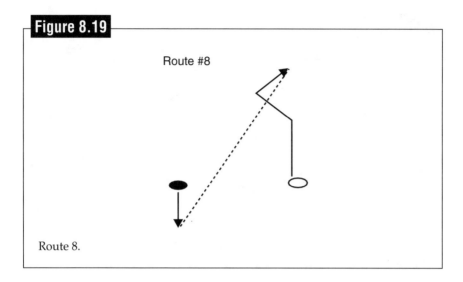

Figure 8.19

Route #8

Route 8.

step-up action ensures a full range of motion for the throw. If the quarterback can't drop eight yards deep in five steps, he should take seven shorter steps on the drop to gain the needed distance from the line of scrimmage. During the drop, the ball should be carried at the base of the numbers. The quarterback keeps two hands on the football until his nonthrowing hand leaves the ball in the natural throwing motion. The quarterback false keys the deep secondary with a look-off action in the drop. The field general needs to key the corner or safety (if two deep) to determine where the football will be thrown.

Coaching points—The quarterback must either throw this route up and over or lead the receiver back to the sideline. This play is super against a three-deep zone or two-deep/man-under zone, so long as the quarterback reads the receiver's go or break off. If used versus double-zone cover, a second receiver runs a complementary out route (2 or 4) under the 8 play to more easily exploit the corner. Also, this route can be used in connection with roll-out, sprint, or bootleg action.

Route 9

Route—The receiver must begin the route as if he is on a vertical designed path and break to a read/post at about 10 yards upfield. The receiver runs at the free safety (or split if two safeties) by way of his route. The receiver determines whether to go all the way to the post or break off and settle on his fifth step off the stem.

Figure 8.20

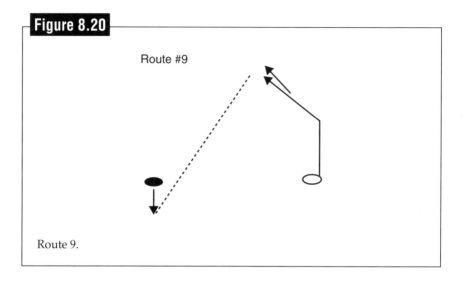

Route #9

Route 9.

Quarterback technique—The quarterback reads the free safety or safeties (if two) for depth to determine when and where to throw the ball. A drop of five large steps or modified seven-step drop should be used. During the drop, the ball should be carried number high. The quarterback should push off his plant foot and step up in the direction of the desired receiving spot. He must throw over the top if the receiver is behind the defender. If not, a harder line drive pass is used. Because the route is out of reach of the under cover, there is no need to key or read through. Instead the quarterback focuses on the deep middle third of the field, reading the deep cover to the receiver's adjustment. Maximum depth on setup helps with the necessary vision for this play.

Coaching points—The depth of the free safety or safeties is the best indicator for the quarterback to determine if a 9 route will go deep or settle. The route can be used against any coverage (zone or man). A speedy receiver adds a new dimension to the play. The 9 route is better when used from a spread formation, with an outside receiver running the play, and enhanced when an inside receiver runs a clearing zero route. Maximum protection (seven or eight blocking) ensures the time needed for this 3- to 3 1/2-second route.

Route Zero

Route—The zero route is the home run path on the tree. The receiver should use an outside release and stretch the cover inside out by running near the sideline. He must use his acceleration to get by the defender. At the 6 and 7 route levels, a fake or change of gait can influence the defensive back to think a cut or break is about to be made.

Quarterback technique—Rhythm is the critical aspect of this play. On a five-step drop, the quarterback sets his back foot and gets the ball off. The ball must be thrown up and over the top against the sideline. He must follow through by stepping up in the direction of the pass. The quarterback must always lead the receiver so that the ball position is his against the defender. A zero pass play should be thrown to the intended receiver 20 to 25 yards from the line of scrimmage, as a longer throw often lowers the percentage rate for completion. A good back foot push off helps the accuracy of this pass. The quarterback's back-side shoulder should drop and his lead arm extend to aid rhythm. A full hip rotation is important when throwing a zero route.

Coaching points—The zero route is better and easier when it's thrown to the field, but the football must be passed in rhythm on the fifth step plant. Always attempt to match up (by formation use) the best and fastest receiver against the worst, slowest corner. Throwing this pass on first down deep in your territory or just after a turnover brings the best results. If the defense is using a double safety roll-up corner, the zero route needs to be thrown hard, flat, and between the two defenders against the sideline.

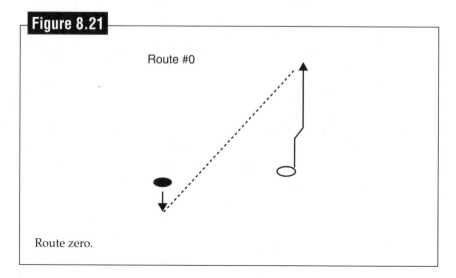

Figure 8.21

Route #0

Route zero.

Pattern Combinations

Combine tree routes that complement each other to make sound pass patterns. Use numbers when incorporating two routes to call the play. For example, combining the 2 and 5 routes makes a 25 pattern, in which the second receiver from the sideline executes a 2 route and the widest player in the formation runs a 5 route (see figure 8.22). Other sample combinations are 28, 44, 09, 57, and 85.

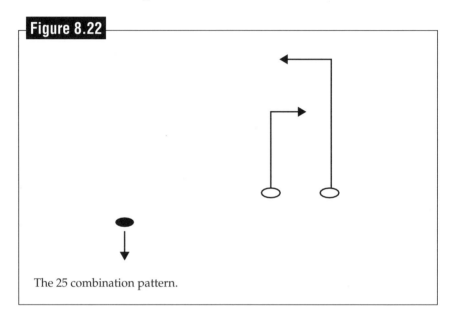

Figure 8.22

The 25 combination pattern.

When three or more routes are combined, it's best to identify the play with a word instead of numbers. Any catchy or descriptive word can be used, for example, "flood," "layer," "divide," "under," "cross," and so on.

Regardless of the pass play's design, the tree serves as the source for the pattern. The passing tree is the foundation from which the passing game evolves. The quarterback's being able to throw these 10 significant routes with precision is everything to a team's passing effectiveness. Packaging receivers for a play combining specific tree routes makes up a pattern. Most pass offenses have two-, three-, and four-man patterns derived from the basic tree.

Choice Passing

Another type of passing merits mentioning and can be an important part of a pass offense. In recent years, passing attacks have employed a new twist, which has added a lot to the offense. Perhaps the most noteworthy is the choice passing play. The play is built around a given receiver having the option of breaking his route off one direction or another. Which way the receiver goes is based on his read of the defender whom he is working against at the time.

Because the direction of the final cut of the route is unknown before the snap, the play called in the huddle or at the line of scrimmage is called using the word "choice." For example, the quarterback would call this type of pass play by calling the intended receiver's football name and adding the word "choice." If the desired receiver is a tight end, the play could be called tight end choice. If the predetermined receiver is a flanker, the call would be flanker choice. Because most teams use letters to represent positions—such as X, Z, Y, H, S, and so on—it's appropriate to precede the word "choice" with the letter representing the position. Thus, the call might be Y choice or Z choice.

A typical choice route would be to use Y as the receiver on a 12-yard in or out. The read to determine choice would be the nearest inside linebacker to the Y position's side of the formation. This particular play is recommended against a three-linebacker system. The key is the middle linebacker. If the middle linebacker drops straight back or away from the tight end, the Y runs an in route. If the middle linebacker drops to the Y side of the formation, the Y runs an out route (figure 8.23).

To assist the choice route, a back should be assigned to run a swing route away from Y. This manuever may or may not influence the drop of the middle linebacker, but it likely will free him to go one way or the other. This will make the read for both the quarterback and the tight end easier. In the following diagrams, the key and choice process is presented.

Another choice route is the Z choice (figure 8.24). The key on this route is either the depth of or shade of the corner. A choice is made at five yards, as to running a slant or sideline pass, depending on

Figure 8.23

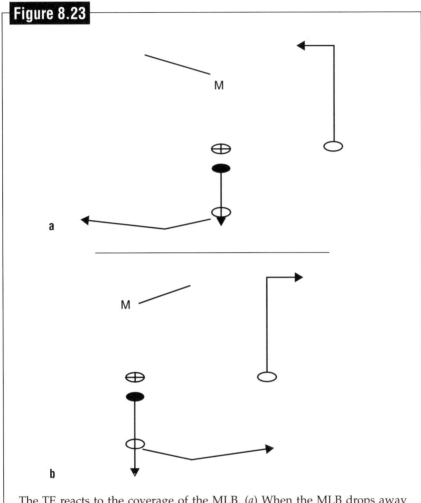

The TE reacts to the coverage of the MLB. (*a*) When the MLB drops away from the TE, the TE runs an in route. (*b*) When the MLB comes toward the TE, he runs an out route.

the shade or depth of the corner. If the corner is off more than seven yards and has an outside shade, a slant is executed. Should the corner be aligned inside of the Z and off eight or more yards, an out is run. When a corner is stationed closer than six yards to the Z, a fade route is executed, as long as the shade is on the inside. If the shade is outside and the distance off the Z is fewer than six yards, a drive slant technique route is executed.

Figure 8.24

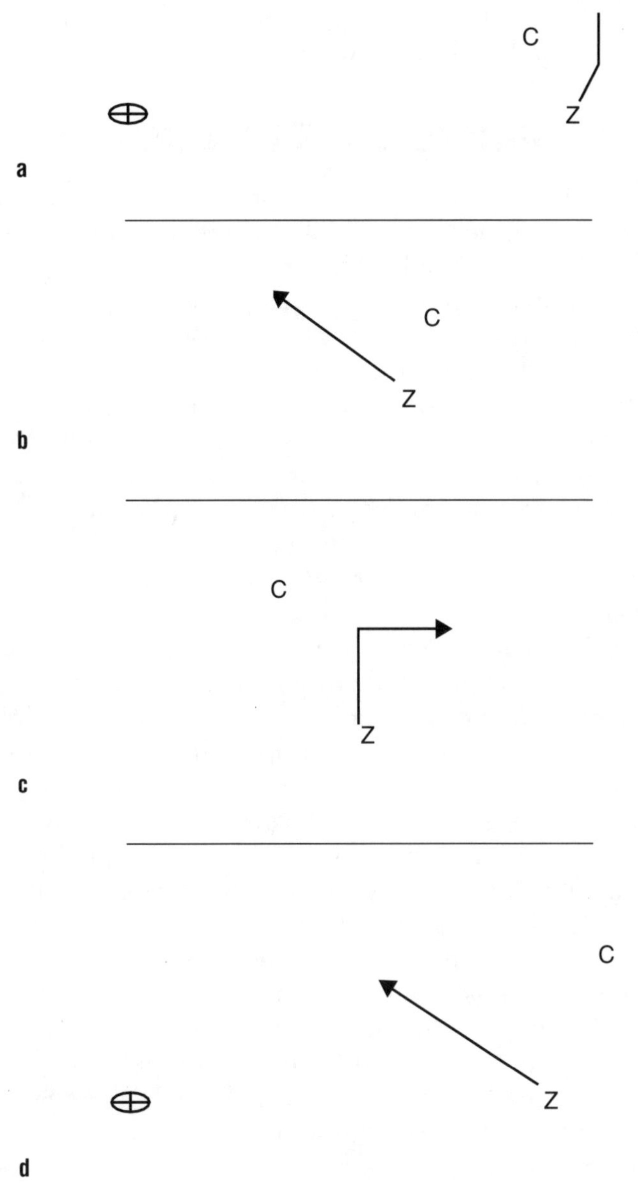

The Z choice. Fewer than six yards off the LOS: (*a*) inside shade and (*b*) outside shade. Nine or more yards off the LOS: (*c*) inside shade and (*d*) outside shade.

Regardless of the type of choice route and receiver used, the quarterback, like the receiver, has to make the correct read, or the play will fail. A bad read by either the receiver or the quarterback too often results in an interception. Conversely, a correct read, route, throw, and catch can be a highly successful play.

Complete Pass Offense

A complete passing attack is made up of both rhythm and disciplined passes. The quarterback's ability to execute both of these assignments equally well is not likely. Throwing disciplined passes is very complex and more difficult to develop.

The solution is a system that adopts what the quarterback does best as the basis of the passing offense and sprinkles in what is more difficult for him. It's safe to say that most quarterbacks are superior at rhythm throwing and many offenses are geared around this aspect of pass offense.

There are some good examples of rhythm passing quarterbacks. Who can forget the finely tuned rhythm passing of Dan Fouts to Kellen Winslow? Joe Montana to Jerry Rice was another fantastic hook up. Four Super Bowl appearances showcased the great talent of Terry Bradshaw and Lynn Swan. Yes, on all levels—high school, college, and professional—there is and always has been unstoppable quarterback–receiver rhythm pass combinations. Consistent, disciplined passers are fewer in number, but the popularity of the West Coast style of attack has increased and perfected disciplined passing.

This chapter has covered a lot of information about throwing the football. We have explored the how and why of both rhythm and disciplined passing. The intent has been to provide insight and technique to deal with throwing the ball effectively.

The distinctions between rhythm and disciplined passes are striking. A quarterback needs to understand and use both of these aspects of a passing attack. More important than classification is application. When a team's quarterback can competently execute rhythm and disciplined throwing, the team has a complete passing attack. When he can't, the team has a limited passing attack. Limited may not be bad, however, as doing a few things well is better than attempting a multitude ineffectively. The quarterback's passing skills, as they relate to his ability to throw disciplined and rhythm passes, determine the team's pass offense.

CHAPTER 9

PASS SITUATION READS

Pass situation reads are at the heart of effectively completing passes. Incorrect assessments, whether from blitz or coverage, almost always lead to one of the three no-nos for a quarterback: getting sacked, throwing an incomplete pass, or giving up an interception. In this chapter, we analyze these quarterback nightmares, focusing on how to avoid them.

Within a system of pass offense, a quarterback has to do his own thing. He must use his personal ingenuity and physical assets to recognize and attack coverage. Reading cover is somewhat specific as to where, when, and how. Recognizing zone or man coverage is always the focal point for effective pass execution.

Anticipating coverage also is extremely beneficial for reliable play selection. The design of the football field and the formations used by the offense dictate probable coverage. Even with this predetermined information, the quarterback still must zero in on an area or person in the secondary to make a decision as to whom to throw to, when, and where.

Pass rush, line stunts, and blitz dictate the type of coverage a defense uses. The quarterback's timing of a throw depends on handling these factors. The signal caller often must change his key or read because of the restricted time allowed by the pass rushers.

The width of a football field is divided into thirds (depending on the level of competition). This affects the working room for a pass offense, which affects the type of patterns to be used. As an offense moves downfield, the limited vertical distance also restricts the nature of passing routes.

Pass protection style and quality influence the type of pass patterns and passing action employed. These factors influence both the keying and reading processes. The physical and mental makeup of the quarterback determine to a great extent the style of pass protection used.

There are many factors to assessing coverage. Knowledge about specific coverages brings a wealth of potentially positive choices to a quarterback. If he can break down coverage, the field general has a chance to beat it. Successful quarterbacks in a passing scheme generally are effective at overcoming coverage and completing passes. They have learned to simplify the complexity of coverage by making good evaluations. A cunning quarterback, well gifted in understanding and possessing a degree of skill, can operate with great ease, confidence, and success against almost any form of coverage.

To humble a defensive secondary is to exploit it by consequential achievements. Subdue a secondary and you conquer it. The best way to accomplish this is to have accurate, consistent reads in the passing game.

Reading the Secondary

Reading coverage is like locating a place on a map. Some quarterbacks find the spot quickly, while others struggle to identify it at all. Reading secondary coverage alignment to determine coverage is the first step for a signal caller toward establishing a productive pass play. This process is best done by identifying specifics within the makeup of the opposition's secondary. Clues are broken down into presnap evaluation, followed by recognition during the play's development. Even though every defense employs many common forms of coverage, how each team uses these coverages is somewhat unique unto itself. This is understandable when you consider how personnel, coaching philosophy, field position, hash marks, score, and time on the clock influence decisions. Even the condition of the field (hard, soft, or wet) may affect the nature and type of coverage a defense exhibits in a game.

Therefore, nothing is etched in stone when it comes to anticipating what a defense will do coverage wise; there are only indicators. Identifying coverage seems even more difficult when you realize

Houdini on the Field

Courtesy of Don Read

In 1993, the University of Montana's quarterback, Dave Dickenson—now with the San Diego Chargers—was a master at flashing head and eye fakes. He could move defenders where he wanted better than most quarterbacks, allowing his receivers to get open. After a game between the University of Montana and the University of Oregon, Rich Brooks, coach of the Ducks, nicknamed Dickenson "Houdini." Reading coverage and influencing it are critical for a successful passing attack.

that potential coverage often changes just prior to the snap or during the play. From the defense's point of view, the key to defending the forward pass is to make the quarterback throw when he doesn't want to or throw to someone he doesn't want to throw to.

With all the possible difficulties that confront a quarterback when he passes the ball, it is understandable when he is unsuccessful. Add to this the other major obstacle of incorrectly determining coverage, and the result is often a catastrophe. The difficulties become even more complex when offensive personnel other than the quarterback, and their potential for error, are added to the mix.

Because of these factors, it is easy to comprehend why most people connected with the game appreciate this aspect of the quarterback. His ability to perceive and react correctly to various coverages is perhaps his biggest challenge. Mastery of these skills is difficult for many and demanding for all quarterbacks.

To simplify teaching and to provide an easy index for classifying secondary alignments, coverage is broken down into three general categories: zone, man-to-man, or combination coverages. These classifications present a clearer picture of coverage strengths, allowing for recognizing the weakness contained in each form of coverage.

Every coverage has its advantages and disadvantages. Most defenses defend the opposition first with coverage that will best resist whatever an offense's personnel and formations present. With this in mind, we examine the common coverages that most often confront a quarterback. To know these coverages and their intricacies is to be able to exploit them.

Zone Coverage

In zone coverage, defensive backs, linebackers, and occasionally a lineman defend receivers within a predetermined assigned area of the field. Generally, there are only two forms of zone coverage: two deep and three deep. In two-deep zone coverage (figure 9.1), two defenders (usually safeties) defend the football field beyond linebacker range or drop, dividing the playing surface in half, providing deep coverage. Three-deep coverage (figure 9.2) uses three defensive backs, each responsible for defending against receivers in one-third of the field beyond linebacker coverage alignment. All other forms of deep zone coverage are a preplay or in-progress play development rotation from two or three deep (figure 9.3).

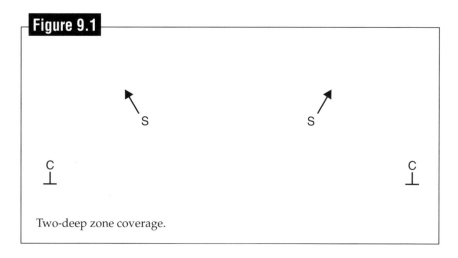

Figure 9.1

Two-deep zone coverage.

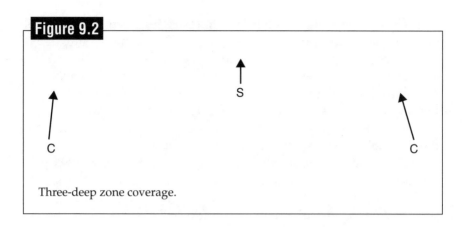

Figure 9.2

Three-deep zone coverage.

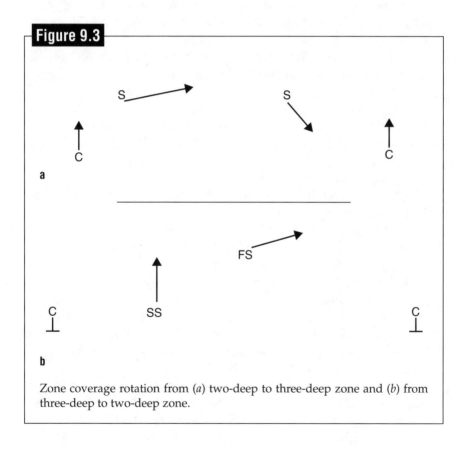

Figure 9.3

a

b

Zone coverage rotation from (*a*) two-deep to three-deep zone and (*b*) from three-deep to two-deep zone.

The shorter-coverage defenders (linebackers) in front of the two- or three-deep zone vary in number, depending on how many defensive linemen are placed along the front. The defense used determines how many linebackers are available for coverage responsibility. Normally most teams present a three-, four-, or five-man front, allowing for eight, seven, or six defenders to be used as zone pass defenders. The short zones (in front of deep cover) are divided among the linebackers or a safety or corner to defend.

The number of undercover deep defenders (two or three) determines the nature of zone cover to a great extent. Those not assigned to deep coverage or shallow zone cover make up the designated pass rushers. A particular defense can add rushers or coverage people as dictated by offensive formations or by choice.

This area of the playing field (line of scrimmage to about 15 yards deep) is where most passes are thrown and completed. Therefore, linebackers need to be not only good run stoppers but also solid pass defenders. Quarterbacks should always try to exploit this intermediate coverage area and the personnel within it. Passes thrown here are shorter and thus are higher-percentage throws.

Some pass patterns are far more effective versus zone cover and thus manifest themselves, depending on the specific type of zone defense presented. This allows some ideal passing plays to be used. The challenge is to recognize the coverage so that the appropriate play can be used at the correct time.

On most plays, after identifying the coverage prior to the snap, the quarterback will focus on a certain defender within the zone to determine where the football will be thrown. He does not concentrate on his receivers (though there are some exceptions). Similar to his awareness of where pass rushers are, the quarterback must see his receivers but not zero in on them visibly when throwing versus zone coverage. Figures 9.1 through 9.6 illustrate zone coverages. A careful look at these secondary alignments and defended areas dramatizes the vulnerability of each form of coverage (figures 9.4 and 9.5). The areas within the zone coverage package that can be taken advantage of will be discussed shortly.

Many defenses will not line up presnap in such a way that shows the quarterback their intent to be two or three deep. The quarterback often has to deal with late changes. Late adjustments in deep coverage are an attempt to confuse the quarterback's reads and keys. The purpose of late-changing alignment, however, is not only to confuse the quarterback but to delay or alter his decisions as to when and to whom the football is thrown.

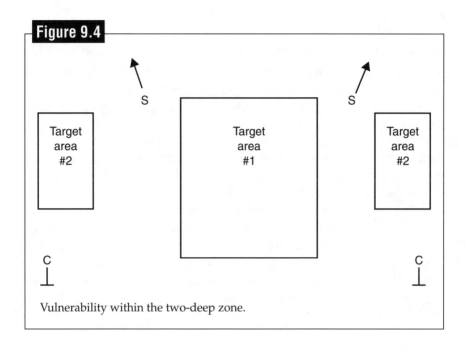

Vulnerability within the two-deep zone.

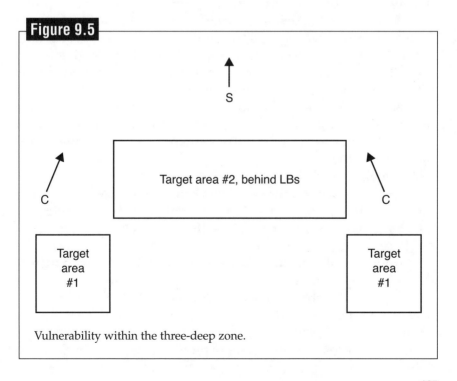

Vulnerability within the three-deep zone.

Reading

Figures 9.4 and 9.5 identified target areas versus zone coverage and indicated inherent weaknesses in these alignments. The quarterback reads the pass defenders nearest to this vulnerable real estate to be assured that passing lanes are clear. This method helps protect the success of any pass versus zone cover. Many refer to this form of reading as *awareness reading*. To be successful, a quarterback needs excellent peripheral vision, solid understanding of coverage, and good anticipation skills. In general, reading is used when multiple receivers are deployed to a specific area. Sprint or rollout passing, along with bootleg plays, normally also requires reading for the quarterback.

Another popular pass play in which the quarterback reads versus zone is when a receiver runs a route under the deep coverage, focusing on the drop of the linebacker. The quarterback looks for the natural holes created within the coverage made by the linebacker's drop. The receiver also looks for natural holes created by the under cover in zone coverage.

Keying

A second way for the quarterback to determine where and when to throw the ball is by keying. Keying refers to isolating a defender within the zone coverage and hopefully defeating him with a route or two-man pattern. An example would be when running a curl route. The quarterback focuses on a defender while his receiver curls behind and slides away from him, usually to the inside, placing the defensive player out of position (figure 9.6). The defender then is unable to get to the throw. Keying might also involve focusing on a corner while two receivers execute sideline routes to determine which receiver gets the ball.

A combination of keying and reading can be used with a layer concept when two or more receivers run routes across the field in the face of the quarterback at different depths, allowing him to pick which receiver to throw to based on the space between the defenders. Receivers can also run routes in the same direction or cross the field from opposite sides. In the process of combo evaluating, a signal caller may zero in on a defender or just scan for a hole in the coverage. Combination assessing is less frequently used and requires a lot of experience to perfect.

The reading or keying approach should be used on almost all routes or patterns. It is important to provide the quarterback ample

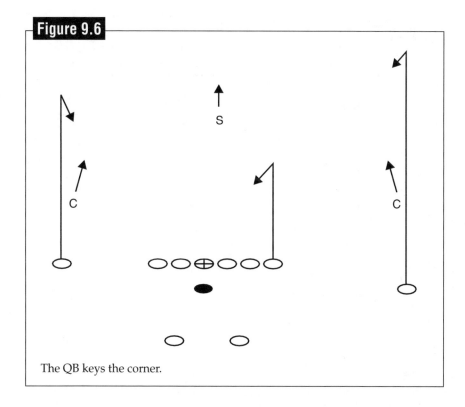

Figure 9.6

The QB keys the corner.

practice time to master this phase of the passing game. In all passing against coverage in practice, the quarterback should focus on the key. Breaking zone coverages down into parts for the quarterback aids in his learning to defeat various secondary alignments. A quarterback is influenced the most by his mistakes. It is therefore better to execute these mistakes in practice than on game day. Practicing keying and reading leads to development of the skill.

Man-to-Man Coverage

Unlike zone coverage, in which defensive players defend designated areas of the field, in man coverage a defender covers a receiver/back regardless of where this offensive player goes. The keying or reading process used versus zone cover is not valid versus man cover.

When working versus man cover, the challenge for the field general is to set up and locate the best matchup possible via a given route (see figure 9.7). The formation, or the use of motion, can often assist the quarterback in getting the desired matchup. The

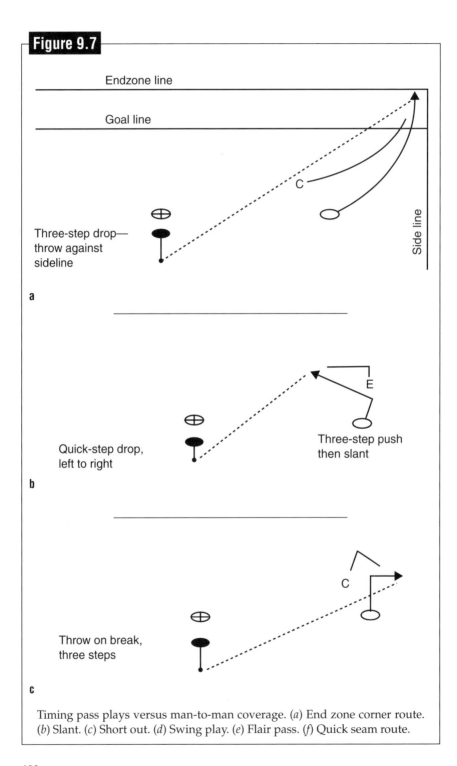

Figure 9.7

Endzone line

Goal line

Side line

Three-step drop—
throw against
sideline

C

a

Quick-step drop,
left to right

Three-step push
then slant

E

b

Throw on break,
three steps

C

c

Timing pass plays versus man-to-man coverage. (*a*) End zone corner route.
(*b*) Slant. (*c*) Short out. (*d*) Swing play. (*e*) Flair pass. (*f*) Quick seam route.

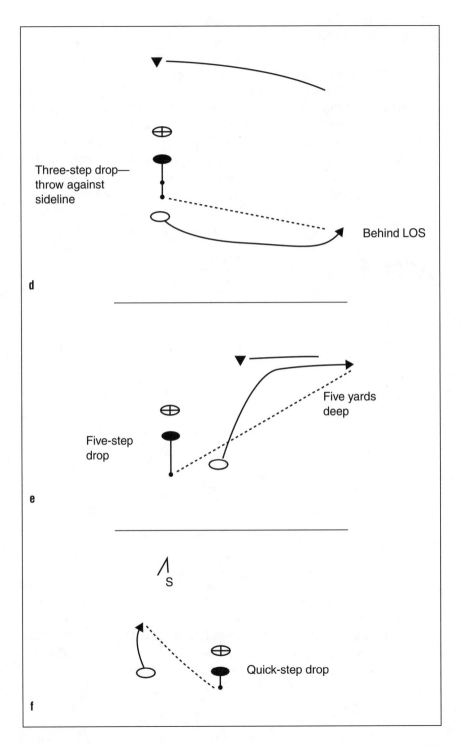

Three-step drop—
throw against
sideline

Behind LOS

d

Five-step
drop

Five yards
deep

e

S

Quick-step drop

f

receiver's position relative to a defender and the quarterback's ability to get the ball to the receiver at a given time and place are critical.

Throwing against man-to-man coverage highlights timing and accuracy, in contrast to throwing the ball where the defender is not, as in zone coverage. The ongoing challenge is to try to get the most qualified receiver working against the poorest defender when attacking man cover. Another approach is to work speed by crossing or vertical design routes to physically outrun a defender using man-to-man coverage. Both these approaches are sound and frequently employed against man-to-man coverage. Examples of throwing on the break are shown in figure 9.8. The steps a quarterback needs to allow for on break delivery are determined by the route.

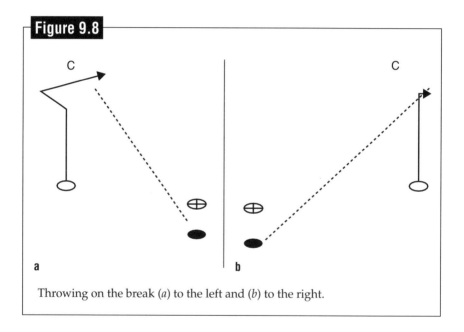

Figure 9.8

Throwing on the break (*a*) to the left and (*b*) to the right.

It makes good sense then to choose timing routes to overcome man coverage. Timing pass plays requires the quarterback to throw the ball to a given place on the field, coordinating his steps and setup with those of the receivers. These kinds of plays are end zone corner routes, slants, short outs, swings, flair passes, and quick seam routes.

Man coverage can also be exploited by the use of multiple cut routes because the defender in man cover often gets turned around or loses his connection to the receiver. The term generally used to describe the nature of this approach to passing is spot passing or throwing on the break.

In general, there are two forms of man-to-man coverage. Pure man coverage involves locking every secondary/linebacker on an offensive receiver or running back. The quarterback can anticipate more blitzing when the defense plays this form of coverage. He also can know there is little if any chance for double coverage. The second style of man coverage is man/free (figure 9.9). This coverage allows for an extra secondary defender to be free for double coverage or for playing deep routes. A quarterback has to be aware of the free safety in this coverage. Figure 9.9 shows a three-deep free safety form of coverage to emphasize where the free safety is located.

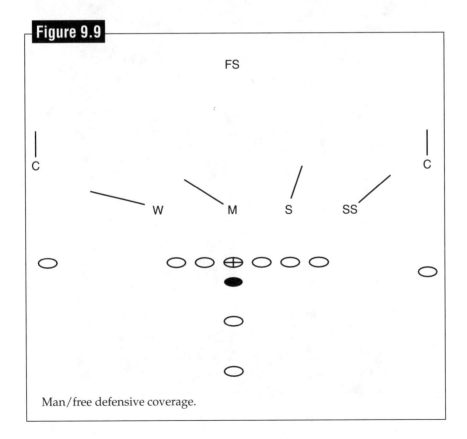

Figure 9.9

Man/free defensive coverage.

Combination Coverage

Combination coverage is much more complicated and difficult to defeat through reading, keying, or timing. Combination coverage may combine man and zone tactics or use refinements within the strength of these coverages. When zone and man coverage are used together, they create the ultimate defense against a great pass catcher or a group of receivers. To compensate when the ball is on a hash mark, a defense often presents a form of combination coverage. These are only two situations in which a team might use combo cover.

© G. Newman Lowrance

■ Peyton Manning changes the play at the line of scrimmage. After reading the pass coverage, the quarterback can switch to a play that gives the offense the advantage against the coverage shown.

Playing a person man-to-man while applying zone against the rest of the opponents is the premise of mixing the two basic coverages. When the ball is on the hash mark, a wide side and short side are created, so some coaches might choose to use man cover to the short side and zone to the wide field unless the offense places multiple receivers to the short side. The sideline itself curtails the functionability of a receiver, restricting the routes that can be run.

A popular tactic used within combination coverage is to change from man cover to zone or switch the men being covered within the man cover package after the ball comes up. This method of bracketing, or passing off responsibility from one defender to another, is frequently incorporated when an offensive team crosses two detached receivers or an inside receiver runs an out route and an outside receiver runs an in route. Bracketing can also provide double cover on a receiver if the receiver is running a pattern between them.

No doubt, more interceptions are thrown against combination coverage than any other form of coverage. Rather than try to figure out whom to read and how to execute against this defense, it's a good rule of thumb to prepare specific patterns to use against a team that features combo coverage more than 25 percent of the time. Plays that stretch the coverage in particular can best attack the one-on-one defender with your best receiver. Carefully designed strategy can create a mismatch with the defense, forcing a bracket or exchange-type cover. Using motion often bolsters an offensive attack versus combo coverage, as it forces the defense to change responsibilities, providing easier determination of the defensive adjustment and to whom to throw the football.

A team cannot spend enough practice time readying itself for this kind of a secondary play. One suggestion to get the opposition out of this coverage is to simplify the read or key for the quarterback. Implementing various types of man-in-motion plays will provide an offense with desired coverage, making the task of the quarterback easier.

A Quarterback's Confidence

Regardless of the type of coverage a quarterback faces, he should believe it can be defeated. The solution is to have predetermined concepts about coverage reads and keying and spend adequate practice time applying this knowledge. Throwing to the primary, secondary, and safety valve receivers in each pattern in a sequence over and over in practice develops this aspect of passing. The quarterback also can accomplish a lot of skill in identification and planning for overcoming individual coverages through studying films in the off-season. Chapter 14 examines the quarterback's involvement in coverage study.

Other than fieldwork and studying videotapes, the most helpful aid to assist in coverage recognition and defeating it is the absorption of a keying the coverage chart (tables 9.1, 9.2, and 9.3). These charts identify and isolate the principal keys a field general needs to recognize once the ball comes up. In short, they break down the coverage into what to look at to determine when and where the football is to be thrown. These charts simplify the learning process for the signal caller by connecting routes and patterns, presnap reads, and primary keys. Keying the coverage charts can be likened to offensive linemen using rules to the blocking scheme. The value of keying the coverage charts is that they become the resource from which the signal caller can draw as needed.

Remember not all routes or patterns are good against every form of coverage. In this chapter, we have explored only the most common coverages used today and some reads and keys to attack their weaknesses. The quarterback's job is to go beyond these basic concepts and alter the execution to fit the needs of his particular pass offense. To succeed in defeating coverages, the quarterback must recognize what he is up against, key and read correctly, and ad lib when necessary.

It's a good idea for the quarterback to go slow when digesting a pass offense's keying and reading. The quarterback must absorb only what he can handle at a given time. Improved offensive productivity is around the corner for every quarterback, and it's not difficult to achieve with appropriate planning, thought, and organization. Coverage assessments are essential and fundamental to a passing attack. The quarterback must master this skill to effectively defeat defensive coverage.

Table 9.1 Keying the Coverage Chart: Three Deep

Basic pass routes	Presnap reads	Primary key
Curl		
Inside wide receiver	Three deep	Linebacker
Outside wide receiver	Three deep	Alley defender
Post	Three deep	Outside deep defender
Sideline		
Under 10 yards	Three deep	Alley defender
Over 10 yards	Three deep	Outside deep defender
Slant		
Outside wide receiver	Three deep	Alley defender
Inside wide receiver	Three deep	Linebackers
Flag	Three deep	Outside deep defender
Hitch	Three deep	Outside defender
Crossing route		
Under 15 yards	Three deep	Linebacker
Over 15 yards	Three deep	Inside and outside deep defenders
Seam		
Inside wide receiver	Three deep	Linebacker
Outside wide receiver	Three deep	Alley defender
Streak		
Inside wide receiver	Three deep	Inside deep defender
Outside wide receiver	Three deep	Outside deep defender
Circle	Three deep	Linebackers
Drag	Three deep	Linebackers
Flat	Three deep	Alley defenders

Table 9.2　Keying the Coverage Chart: Two Deep

Basic pass routes	Presnap reads	Primary key
Curl		
Inside wide receiver	Two deep	Linebacker
Outside wide receiver	Two deep	Alley defender
Post	Two deep	Outside deep defender
Sideline		
Under 10 yards	Two deep	Outside short defender
Over 10 yards	Two deep	Outside short defender
Slant		
Outside wide receiver	Two deep	Alley defender
Inside wide receiver	Two deep	Linebackers
Flag	Two deep	Outside deep defender
Hitch	Two deep	Outside defender
Crossing route		
Under 15 yards	Two deep	Linebacker
Over 15 yards	Two deep	Inside and outside deep defenders
Seam		
Inside wide receiver	Two deep	Linebacker
Outside wide receiver	Two deep	Alley defender
Streak		
Inside wide receiver	Two deep	Inside deep defender
Outside wide receiver	Two deep	Outside deep defender
Circle	Two deep	Linebackers
Drag	Two deep	Linebackers
Flat	Two deep	Alley defenders

Table 9.3   Keying the Coverage Chart: Man-to-Man

Basic pass routes	Presnap reads	Primary key
Curl		
Inside wide receiver	Man	Cover man
Outside wide receiver	Man	Cover man/linebacker
Post	Man	Cover man/free safety
Sideline		
Under 10 yards	Man	Cover man
Over 10 yards	Man	Cover man
Slant		
Outside wide receiver	Man	Cover man/alley defender
Inside wide receiver	Man	Cover man/linebackers
Flag	Man	Cover man
Hitch	Man	Cover man
Crossing route		
Under 15 yards	Man	Cover man/linebacker
Over 15 yards	Man	Cover man/linebacker
Seam		
Inside wide receiver	Man	Cover man/linebacker
Outside wide receiver	Man	Cover man/alley defender
Streak		
Inside wide receiver	Man	Cover man/free safety
Outside wide receiver	Man	Cover man
Circle	Man	Cover man/linebackers
Drag	Man	Cover man/linebackers
Flat	Man	Cover man

Looking for the Blitz

Fronts often provide telling clues as to probable coverage. Quarterbacks should be conscious of the number of defensive linemen, as well as linebackers in the game. Coverages are somewhat fused to the number of defenders in the defensive box and how they are aligned. Normally, the more defenders on the line of scrimmage, the more likely the coverage is man to man. Fewer defenders along the line of scrimmage is a possible indication the coverage will be a form of zone.

Because the number of defenders on the line of scrimmage isn't an absolutely determining factor, the quarterback needs to look for other clues. For example, the width or depth of the linebackers informs the signal caller if, where, and how these defenders might be positioned in the coverage. Linebacker position also allows the field general to predict a potential blitz.

Studying videotapes and scouting the tendencies of the opponent's defense are of great value to a quarterback. By identifying fronts and noting the number of defenders in the imaginary box (tight end to tight end), he can predetermine the probability of coverage. This information plus alignment clues also helps predict the likeliness of a blitz.

To beat the blitz, there must be predetermined routes run by receivers on recognition of the blitz. The job of the field general is to get the ball quickly to one of those receivers. Usually the routes are straight upfield, but slants and quick outs can also be used.

Passes in Specific Areas

Defenses tend to play specific coverages in identifiable areas of the field. When you pass the football, many factors play into the strategy for effectively predetermining coverage. These considerations are more pertinent to the experienced signal caller but can be of assistance to the novice quarterback.

One consideration is the appropriate utilization of the playing field. The playing surface is divided into shorter and longer distances to the sideline, affecting the strategy as to the types of formations and plays. As a team works from one goal line to the other, the amount of room for offensive execution changes. How the defense defends is often influenced by field position, forcing the offense to adjust accordingly. A team is required to operate in a field 53 yards wide and 100 yards long, but it's the restrictions within this area that dictate a pass offense. Understanding all the implications within this confinement is paramount to the productivity of an offensive attack.

Regardless of field position, an offense shouldn't adhere to the philosophy that you become run oriented when you're inside your own 10-yard line (green area). Nor should you believe you can't throw the football effectively inside the opponent's 20-yard line (red area). Modify your plays, yes, but don't get away from throwing the ball because of field position. Passing teams have enough trouble running the ball upfield, so why try a ground attack when near the opposition's goal or backed up against your own? It makes little sense, and it won't work. Better by far to live and die doing what you are prepared to do. If that means putting the ball in the air, do so! Mix the run with the pass within a particular offense upfield. This makes good sense and makes an offense more potent. Figure 9.10 shows the field divided into the key zones from goal line to goal line.

Appropriate plays and where to use them on the field are given in the pass offensive area chart (figure 9.11). No one can profess to be correct all the time with successful play calling. The chart should be used only as a guide for selecting plays in a specific area of the field. The quarterback's and team's level of expertise must be a big part of the equation.

The pass offensive area chart (figure 9.11) classifies pass plays and field position. It is an important guide for a quarterback, though it is not to be looked at as an absolute plan. There is good rationale for all plays listed. Use of plays may depend on recent success in the game, down and distance, time on the clock, and score. Which pass to throw and where to throw it should certainly change with the circumstances of the moment. As stated and emphasized in other sections of this text, appropriate play selection has to do with the ability of the team, defensive coverages, fronts, down and distance, and time on the clock.

First downs are important no matter where the football is located. Second downs also are critical in moving the football but are some-what more dictated by the situation. For the signal caller, how he performs on third downs is even more crucial. Regardless of the down, however, the beauty of throwing the ball rather than running it is that 10 yards are always within reach of a well-prepared passing attack. A quarterback passing the ball can treat first, second, or

Figure 9.10

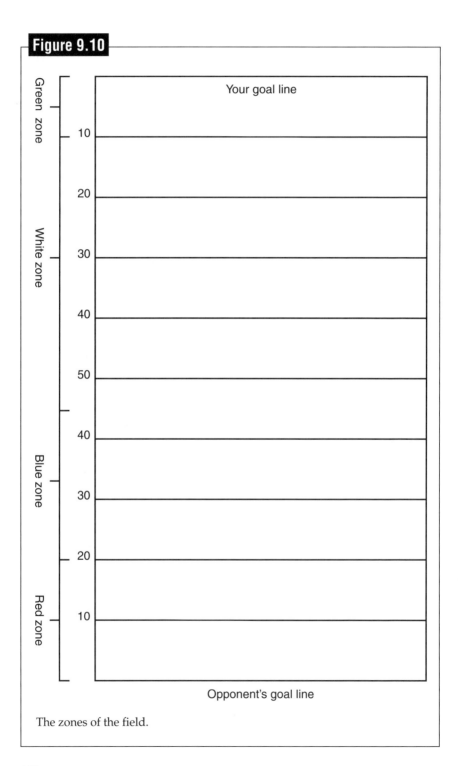

The zones of the field.

Figure 9.11

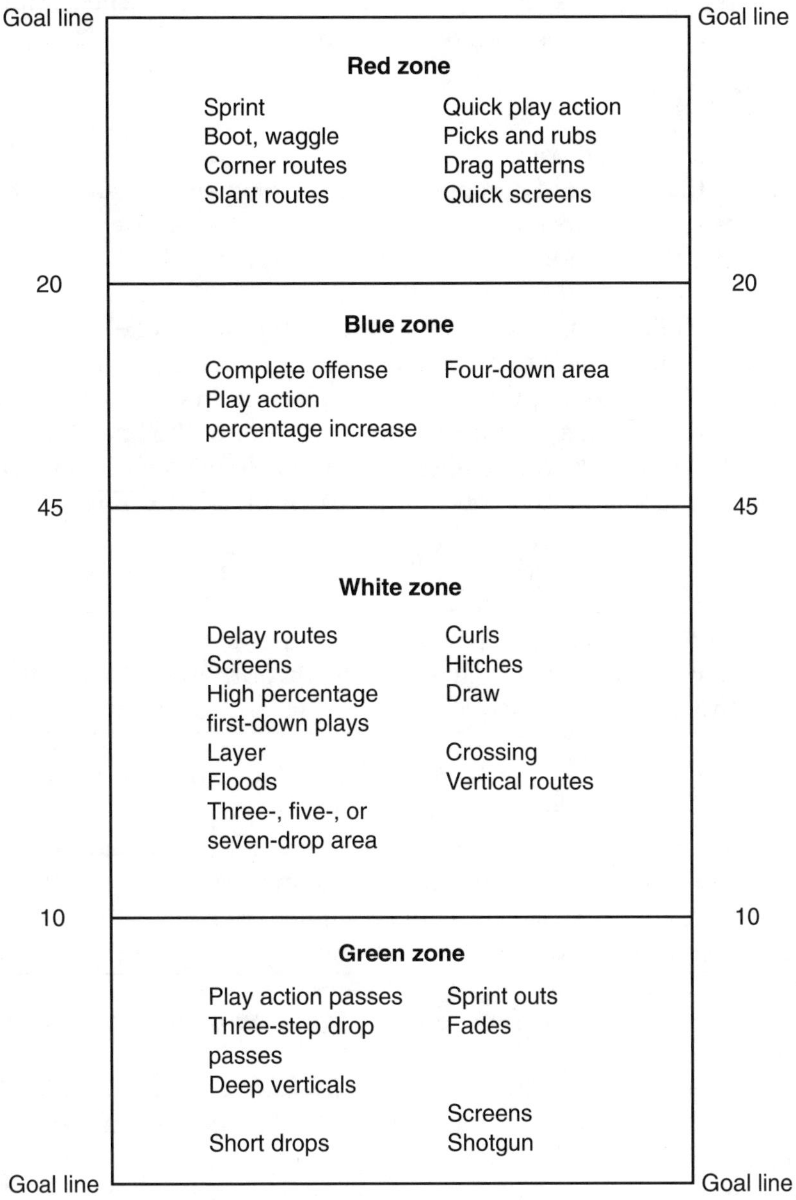

Goal line

Red zone

Sprint	Quick play action
Boot, waggle	Picks and rubs
Corner routes	Drag patterns
Slant routes	Quick screens

20

Blue zone

Complete offense	Four-down area
Play action	
percentage increase	

45

White zone

Delay routes	Curls
Screens	Hitches
High percentage	Draw
first-down plays	
Layer	Crossing
Floods	Vertical routes
Three-, five-, or	
seven-drop area	

10

Green zone

Play action passes	Sprint outs
Three-step drop	Fades
passes	
Deep verticals	
	Screens
Short drops	Shotgun

Goal line

The pass offensive area chart.

third downs the same. The nature of pass plays may vary, depending on the down or the area of the field, but that's all. When you are committed to the pass, the objective is completions; and with completions come first downs and touchdowns.

Red Zone

The red area is the most challenging for an offense. The field shrinks, checking the speed and deception within an offensive package. What becomes very important is raw execution. For the quarterback, this means doing all the little things consistently right. Understanding and adapting to the lack of room in which to run routes is very important. Realize, too, that in this area more blitzing is likely to occur. Coverage will probably favor man-to-man inside the opposition's 20-yard line. The entire defensive secondary counters as an offense draws nearer to the goal line by moving closer to the line of scrimmage. All of these changes allow for better defensive run support and utilization of the end zone line (because of its proximity) as part of the coverage package.

Once in the deep red area—the 10-yard line in—college teams score touchdowns just over 55 percent of the time, on average, while professional clubs in the same field position rate only a little better. These facts vary year in and year out, but basically they prove the value of offensive work in this section of the playing field.

In 1990, after studying the success ratio of teams that I coached for the previous five seasons, I determined our success in the red area was 65 percent. My staff decided to increase our practice time by 20 minutes a week in this area of the field. The end result was that we raised our scoring rate over the next five years to about 70 percent. There is no substitute for committing adequate practice time to the red area. Added emphasis will raise productivity. It's a matter of learning to effectively function in a reduced working space—that's all there is to it.

The major concern that throwing teams must overcome in the red area is the lack of field in which to function. On average, passing teams do not score as often as rushing teams in this area, meaning more practice time and refinement of play selection are needed. As stated earlier, I do not believe that changing to a running team in the red area is an intelligent or productive move.

In theory, the quarterback's passing efficiency rate should improve in the red area because coverage is more predictable (usually man) and the likelihood of getting a heavy dose of blitz can be anticipated. When these are known factors, the quarterback can be better prepared to defeat them. The other advantage for a quarterback passing in the red area is that most defenses will play run first. Effective plays in this area are one-man routes with a single cutting action. Short posts, slants, corner routes, and drags are normally effective in this area versus man coverage.

Blue Zone

The blue area offers an offense everything it can hope for. There is room in which to exploit a defense in terms of both width and depth. In this area, the +45- to +20-yard lines, the offense can operate using all four downs to achieve a first down. Combining room and an extra down is utopia for any passing offense. All plays in the playbook are a go in this particular area of the field.

White Zone

When functioning within the white area, an offense can pull out all the stops and let it all hang out. The difference between the blue and white areas is primarily that there are only three tries to get a first down, or you punt. The white area is located between the −10- and +45-yard lines. To perform successfully in this zone, it's critical to have a high percentage of success on first-down plays. Success here means either a first down or a gain of five yards or more. This enables a coach or quarterback to call for run or pass on second and third downs. The most positive feature of the white area is that the quarterback does not have to worry that a sack will take the team out of field goal range. If it's necessary to punt, the offense still is likely to have good field position when they get the ball back on the next series.

Green Zone

More than in any other position on the field, it is essential to move out of the green area. This delicate territory exists between your goal line and the −10-yard line. Just as it's important to get the football across the goal line in the red area, so is it of major concern to be productive in the green area. Lack of achievement here will likely result in disaster—loss of field position or points on the board for the opposition. The mentality for a quarterback in this area is to get first downs then others.

When deep in your territory, it is critical not to turn the ball over or gain costly penalties. This is not the time to get conservative either. Instead, you need ball movement. A first down or two will take tremendous pressure off your team's defense if they have to take the field because of a punt or turnover. First downs also allow a quarterback to open up and use his total offensive package.

▪ Donovan McNabb escapes from the end zone. In the green zone, a quarterback's primary focus is on moving the ball up the field.

The biggest problems to overcome in the green area are the consequences of a turnover, as well as poor field position if the chains are not moved through offensive execution. For these reasons and more, the green area needs to be treated with the same emphasis addressed in the red area, both philosophically and technically. There is more field in which to work compared to the red area, but the parallel concerns are mirrored in importance with both field positions. Failure in the green area is as bad as no production in the red area. A team that is ineffective in both the red and green areas better be awfully good defensively and have a devastating kicking game.

The following are the quarterback's objectives in the green area:

- To move the ball to reach four-down territory
- To use high-percentage passes (don't be too conservative in play selection)
- To run unexpected plays if appropriate, considering your personnel and the opposition's defensive approach
- To avoid sacks by using the shotgun for maneuverability and vision
- To throw quick passes, using short drops and play action

More than any other place on the gridiron, it is important to remember that the green area requires flawless play from the quarterback. His decision making, checks at the line of scrimmage, use of cadence, and physical performance have tremendous bearing on success or failure, with respect to an offense functioning in this area.

Practice Field Position Concepts

One mistake many quarterbacks make is to try to adapt to play selection on game day. Appropriate play calling and execution need to be refined at early game-week practices.

Practice how it's going to be on game day—what you're going to do, where, when, and how. Surprises should be for the opponent! Build play organization and planning into practice sessions twice a week for plays to be used in that week's game. This type of emphasis is also necessary, with respect to use of formations as they pertain to hash marks and the sideline. The pass offensive area chart (figure 9.11) prepares a quarterback mentally, as well as physically, to exploit the field of play and the team he is about to face.

Sight Adjustment

Regardless of the area of the field, the use of sight adjustments is a valuable weapon. Down and distance, as well as type of coverage, has no bearing on stopping sight adjustment plays. Sight adjustment can defeat any and all coverages anywhere on the gridiron and is why this aspect of passing is so important.

Sight adjusting is that communication between the quarterback and receivers at the line of scrimmage just prior to the snap. The communication normally involves hand signals between the quarterback and receivers. Usually the choice of patterns for the receiver in the sight adjustment package is restricted to three or four routes. The most appropriate are slants, quick outs, hitches, and fade routes. These routes take advantage of any form of cover or defensive alignment. If the defender lines up with an inside shade on the receiver, the sight adjustment will be to an out route or fade. If the alignment of defensive backs favors the outside of the receiver, the call from the receiver will be a slant. If the secondary defender plays off the receiver, the signal will be for a hitch. A press or tight cover would call for a fade route.

A quarterback doesn't have to accept the suggested call of the receiver, as the quarterback makes the final decision. No one else on the team needs to know a sight adjustment play has been signaled, as they block the play called in the huddle.

The advantage of sight adjustments is that the receiver is always right and in the best position for the play called. A coverage that leaves a receiver one-on-one, for example, invites sight adjustment plays. A corner who aligns loosely or presses the receiver can encourage specific sight adjustment calls. Free safeties who line up deep or shallow encourage sight adjustment plays to take advantage of what the center fielder (free safety) is unable to do from his depth.

With sight adjusting built into an offensive system, the pattern selected automatically becomes a high-percentage play. Sight adjusting can be incorporated into an offense with little practice and still be effective. These plays can be used on all downs and anywhere on the grid. One advantage of sight adjusting passing is that it almost eliminates the risk of interceptions or sacks. Though the yardage gained may be minimal, once in a while it turns into a big play. For the signal caller, sight adjustment plays are easy to execute and often are a way out of a bad predetermined call.

Additional Considerations for Elite Passing

Numerous other considerations can surface when it comes to throwing the ball within designated areas. Treatment of these elements must be tempered by the ability of your personnel. Please note the use of the word "tempered," meaning not necessarily eliminated. For example, a quarterback with below-average arm strength may not throw outs into the wide side of the field. The answer for him may be sprinting or rolling out in the direction of the sideline pass, reducing the distance he has to pass the ball.

Maybe the signal caller is young and has difficulty reading coverage or keying. Modification of the ideal needs to be done for him to be successful. An approach could be to throw fewer passes in the middle third of the field, as this is the area most difficult for a young quarterback to deal with. The highest ratio of interceptions occurs here because there are more defenders, regardless of coverage, nearer the football once it is thrown.

Still, another consideration is the opposition's personnel. Sometimes it just makes good sense to stay away from some defensive backs because of their ability. With formation and motion changes, this can be accomplished most of the time without affecting the potential of a desired play. That is to say, you can go the other way or force the talented defensive player to use a different form of coverage or cover someone who is not the primary receiver. In short, creativity within the passing scheme is the name of the game.

When working in any of the four areas on the field, it is wise not to stray from the fundamental guidelines recommended. On the other hand, if an offense is to bring about significant results, it must take advantage of its uniqueness. Each team has its own personality and has to perform accordingly. The quarterback is the catalyst for whatever that personality may be.

Good advice for a quarterback is "You are unequaled with your potential." Potential is the raw material that can evolve into reality with attitude, imagination, time, and commitment. This is particularly true when it comes to pass reads and keying.

Quarterback Protection

Successful passing happens for numerous reasons. Quarterback play as it relates to pass protection is an area of quarterbacking that requires further in-depth study and analysis. To a great extent, protection dictates the nature of the pass offense and affects reading and keying.

There is no passing game without protection. The type of protection influences a signal caller's vision, throwing lanes, follow-through, and types of passing he can use. Poor pass protection for a quarterback can be compared to a fighter getting slammed or soldiers on the front being overwhelmed. An even more descriptive analogy is soldiers on the front losing their air support.

A protection scheme has to take into consideration the quarterback's height, maneuverability, and passing style. Firm, aggressive man or zone protection (figure 9.12a) allows more working room for the quarterback. Cup-type protection (figure 9.12b) encourages the quarterback to step up into the pocket to throw. Slide protection (figure 9.12c) nullifies A, B, and C gap penetration.

Working within the protection is the quarterback's challenge. Understanding the goal and procedure of the blocking pattern allows him to perform at a higher level of efficiency. When the protection is tailored to the quarterback and he to it, an effective pass offense is generated. This alliance not only unites the signal caller and the protection personnel but allows for ongoing adjustments in the scheme as needed. A field general is better at making appropriate reads and decisions when he and his protection mesh.

Calling Audibles

The final section of this chapter ties together all of the information that has been explained so far. Understanding of the material covered to this point is the foundation for a solid audible system, as well as the execution of it.

Audibles are a necessary part of any offensive attack. The audible allows the offense to get away from a bad play or move to a better play. The system needs to be simple yet complete. Any system used is only as effective as the quarterback's ability to evaluate, calculate, and make decisions. This process must be completed in approximately seven seconds, or a delay of game will kick in.

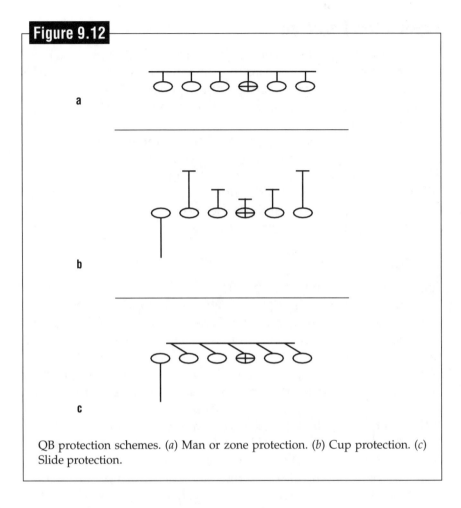

Figure 9.12

a

b

c

QB protection schemes. (*a*) Man or zone protection. (*b*) Cup protection. (*c*) Slide protection.

There are several ways to call automatics. A simple method is to call a live color that indicates that the next play called is a change from what was called in the huddle. If a dead color is called, the play following the dead color means nothing. Regardless of whether the color called is dead or alive, it is barked out twice on the line of scrimmage, once to the left and once to the right, to ensure that everyone heard it. The quarterback can hold his hands in a cup shape around his mouth as he yells the call to further guarantee that the audible is heard.

For example, a quarterback could call an audible using red as the live color. To change the play, he would call "red, red," then the play desired. Because most offensive systems use a numbering system to represent a play, a number would follow the color.

Making the Decision

First, it is most important when calling an audible that play changes go from a run to a run or a pass to a pass. It is to difficult to change a run to a pass or vice versa for all of the personnel that surrounds the quarterback. Blocking changes are much more drastic going from run to pass or pass to run.

The other intelligent thing to do when changing the play is to check to a simpler play rather than a more complex one. By doing this, there is less chance for a mistake. The final thing to know is not to use a man in motion, which complicates timing. The last concern is to stay with the predetermined cadence so as not to increase the potential for individual error.

Changing the Play

There are two distinct reasons for changing a huddle call: if the play called in the huddle appears to be a bad choice once the quarterback sees the defense or if a good play can be changed to a more productive choice based on the defensive alignment. These are good general guidelines, although the ability of the quarterback should influence the latitude he is given. A young, inexperienced quarterback should be restricted to perhaps only checking out of a bad play.

If a run play is called, the field general must analyze the defenders in the tight end to tight end box. He should determine their number, their alignment, and the balance of the defense. The more players in the box or on the side of the run play called, the more perception he must display. Six or seven in the box generally means go with the play called. Eight in the box becomes a larger obstacle. When there are six or seven this near to the line of scrimmage, then the quarterback must determine if the alignment fits with the blocking scheme called. If it does not, he must call an audible.

When a pass play has been selected in the huddle, the role of the quarterback on the line of scrimmage is to concentrate on the potential coverage. He must decide if the pattern selected is good against the likely coverage. He scans the number of defenders in the secondary, their alignment, their distance off the offensive formation, and if it is zone or man coverage. Experienced field generals will look for and see more, such as matchups and defensive huddle adjustments to a formation and, of course, a potential blitz. From his analysis, he must determine to go with the huddle call or choose a

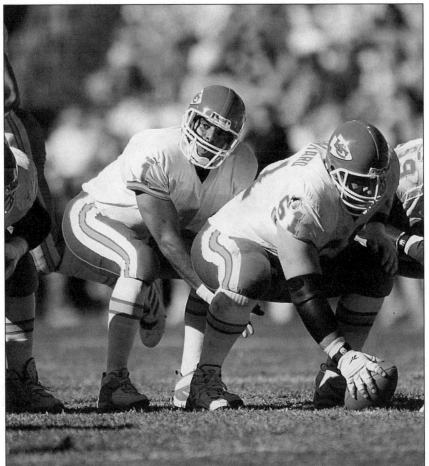

▪ Changing the play at the line of scrimmage requires good communication skills, football intelligence, and the ability to accurately read the defense.

pattern or route that will get the offense out of potential trouble. That is why a coach needs to plan pass plays to beat any coverage and alignment.

Regardless of the play call (run or pass), the key for the quarter-back on the line of scrimmage is to be aware of the time on the clock, the formation called, his personnel, the game conditions, and the score. These elements influence his decision, too, as much as the criteria discussed already. Improper audibles can backfire big time. The idea of the change is to improve the status quo. Drawing in the dirt, so to speak, on the line of scrimmage must not be tolerated.

The primary factor about using any form of audibles is that a quarterback and coach improve the execution of the offense at the line of scrimmage. Practice provides the opportunity to incorporate audibles into existing drills. A team with a quarterback who is confident, knowledgeable, and possesses good common football sense is going to master this process. As is the case in all of quarterbacking, productive execution of any segment of his position leads to a more explosive and effective offense.

CHAPTER 10

GAME PREPARATION

What does game preparation involve from the quarterback's point of view? How important is this preparation for him? When does it all begin?

An all-encompassing game plan considers some basic concerns as well as other not-so-routine subjects. These are factors to consider:

- Probable weather conditions and playing surface
- Personnel matchups
- Factors involving travel and environment
- Mental and psychological concerns
- Injuries (yours and theirs)
- Use of cutups (teaching and highlight videotapes) and/or motivational videotapes
- Efficient bulletin board use
- Theme for this contest
- Leadership for this game
- Big plays (who and how)

Game preparation is primarily in the hands of the coach. Execution of the plan lies to a great extent with the team. The in-between guy in the equation is the quarterback. He must work with both sides and serve the needs of each. A quarterback who understands the many components of the plan is a tremendous asset to making it a reality.

A game plan can be compared to a blueprint for a house. The house will only be suitable if the plan created is precise yet flexible in design. Precise refers to exactly how to do it, and flexible means having the ability to change if and when needed. The coach is like the architect, and the quarterback is like the engineer, working together to ensure the most effective plan possible.

Most battles are won before they are played. John Wooden, one of basketball's all-time great coaches, put it best when he said, "Failure to prepare is preparing to fail!" Inadequate information as to how, when, and where to execute is like a ship without a rudder. Appropriate game planning is every team's edge. For the quarterback, it is the foundation of his performance and execution. In final form, the plan should also provide a clear understanding of how to accomplish game goals.

Contests begin with preparation and end quickly if the preparation is not effective. If the quarterback prepares well, he likely will play well. When the signal caller performs well, the team has a better opportunity of doing the same. Good, constructive game planning is the first step to winning. Without a plan, the team is going nowhere. With a good plan, there is at least a chance to win. Well-conceived and well-executed game plans almost always result in victory.

Yes, game preparation involves sorting out the Xs and Os—and a lot more. Many games are won or lost as a result of game preparation. Preparing for an opponent, when done properly, is a massive job, embracing uncountable details. Because getting ready is so involved and complex, a checklist should be created to ensure that no stone goes unturned (see figure 10.1).

Signal callers have a huge amount to do in preparing for a game. There are videotapes to watch, formations and plays to study, field positions to memorize, and down-and-distance calls to digest. Add learning the opponent's tendencies and personnel to the quarterback's preparation, and we have the weekly mission for each game. For a quarterback to operate on all cylinders, he must be totally plugged in to all aspects of game preparation. The weekly quarterback checklist (figure 10.2) is an excellent source for a quarterback to refer to.

Although the field general doesn't get into analyzing opponents in as broad a spectrum as the coach, he nonetheless ought to have a good idea of what the team is up against each week and how he will fit into the big picture. To accomplish this, he, like the coach, should be able to pinpoint insights to the week's opposition. From these judgments, a game plan is created. Here are the nine insights the quarterback must decipher:

Figure 10.1

_____ Wristbands   _____ Opponent front chart

_____ Clipboards   _____ Opponent coverage charts

_____ Sideline needs   _____ Opponent personnel list

_____ Press box phones   _____ Two-minute offense script

_____ Footballs   _____ Game plan

_____ Grease boards   _____ Pencils and pens

A sample game preparation checklist.

Figure 10.2

_____ Videotape study of the opponent

_____ Red-zone work

_____ Game plan study

_____ Coming-out work

_____ Opponent personnel review

_____ Practice entire game plan

_____ Practice of big plays

A sample weekly quarterback checklist.

1. Study the opponent's philosophy and psychology.
2. Evaluate the opposition's system of play.
3. Determine the quality of the opponent's personnel.
4. Apply pertinent information to the scouting team's preparation.
5. Organize and commit practice time to the plan.
6. Present to the team the how, when, and where aspects of the plan.
7. Use videotape clips of the opponent's fronts and coverages.
8. Videotape practices to evaluate the effectiveness of the plan both early in the week and late.
9. Create supplementary forms to check and evaluate the game plan during the game.

Besides the insights questionnaire, there is another phase of sizing up the team that you are preparing to play. This one is used for a close-up examination of the personality of the enemy. When dissecting the opponent's philosophy, it becomes easier to understand their game plan, as well as their strategy. By asking these questions about the team to be played, you can readily see strengths and weaknesses of the opponent. The following considerations provide additional perception and anticipation of the opposition's probable actions:

- Are they disciplined? In what way?
- What is their organizational structure, with respect to defensive alignment and coverages?
- Does their defensive strength lie with their system or personnel?
- In what ways are they predictable?
- Can they handle formation variations?
- What do they think they have to do to win?
- Who makes their major decisions?
- Is their style conservative or imaginative?
- How do they perform in the second half, on the road or at home, and when behind?
- How does their kicking game mesh with their defense (field position)?
- Who are their defensive leaders?
- Are they an experienced team? At what positions?

© The Sporting Image/Jose Marin

■ Put the strengths of your offense against the weaknesses of the defense.

The answers to these questions help you understand the other team, which helps with overall preparation. Not knowing this data restricts your ability to be ready. Because every contest played is unique, the more you know about your opponent, the easier it is to anticipate what may happen in a game. The scouting report shown in figure 10.3 is a typical compiling of data a quarterback can use as a major resource.

Figure 10.3

Fronts

According to videotape, one or both ends always play up and are containing ends.

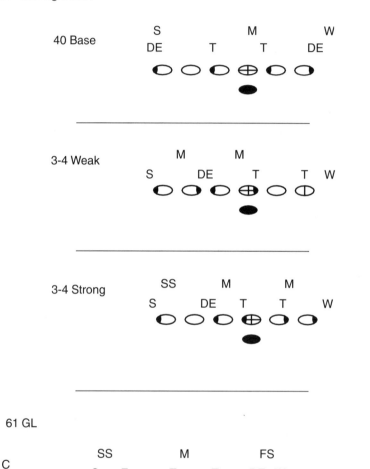

A sample scouting report.

Coverage

Cover 1 Free—92%. FS plays at 10 yards. SS plays at 7 yards. Corners show press and bail. LB's heels are at 4 1/2 yards. Corners will go to receiver strength, and SS will always align on the TE. FS will sneak into the alley on the weak side on rundowns.

Cover 1—2%. FS will cover for the OLB or whoever is blitzing. They will also play this in goal line situations.

They showed little cover 3 and cover 2 against us last year.

Blitzes

Not a strong blitzing team from looking at the videotape—only 16% of the time. But we must prove that we can stop it, nonetheless.

3-4 axe

24 cat

13 cat axe

(continued)

Figure 10.3 *(continued)*

Stunts

Tex

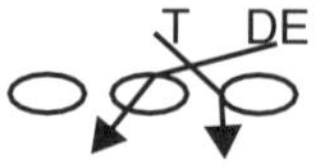

Switch

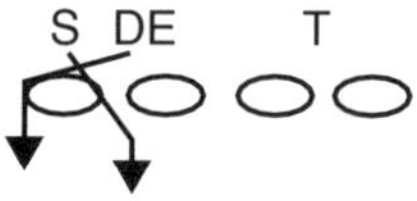

Exit

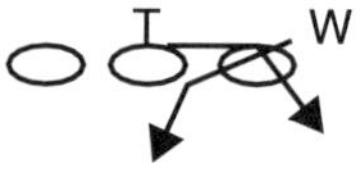

Twist: anytime you have double As

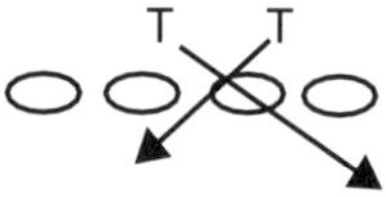

Summary

Down and distance	Fronts	Stunts	Coverage
1st and 10	34 strong–12		
40 base–11	3 axe–1		
Twist–2	1 free–25		
1–1			
2nd and 1–3	34 strong–1	1 free–1	
2nd and 4–6	34 strong–2		
24 weak–1	1 free–3		
2nd and 7 or more	40 base–11		
34 strong–11			
34 weak–1	2 cat–1		
35 A/B–1	1 free–23		
3rd and 1–3	34 strong–3		
43 double eagle–1	Twist–1	1 free–4	
3rd and 4–6	43 base–2		
34 strong–2	2 cat–1	1 free–4	
3rd and 7 or more	34 strong–6		
43 base–5			
34 weak–2	4 blood–1		
3 axe–1			
13 B/A–1			
2 cat–1	1 free–10		
2–1			
1–2			

Evaluating Their System of Defense

You might wonder why it is so important to know the opposition's defensive system of play. There are several answers: to determine strengths and weaknesses; categorize practice emphasis; make decisions on how to place personnel to counter the opponent; and identify defensive formations, alignments, and intricate aspects of the other team.

Once these determinations are made, you proceed to the job of deciding how best to defend and attack the defense. Developing the "how" involves staff meetings to discuss ideas; studying videotapes of the opponent in the off-season, as well as game week; and conversations with coaches of teams the opponent has played or will play. After the raw data are gathered, a large blackboard can be used to record thoughts and potential solutions to be closely examined by all concerned. From this analysis, should come an approach to countering the opposition's style of play and philosophy.

One tip for predicting and dealing with a team using a sophisticated system is "The more complex or multiple their system of attack, the more choices the plan needs to combat it." The opponent's defensive approach can force an offense into detailed preparation to overcome it. For an offense, defensive complexity likely means a different way of attacking.

For example, consider a defensive plan that boasts a wide range of blitzes or multiple coverages. A popular approach to overcome such a challenge is to reduce the formations and plays, cutting down on what can be practiced, which enables what is done offensively to have the best chance of success. Adding a man in motion will influence coverage and even the defensive front alignment to control blitzing. In general, it's best for the quarterback to operate out of a simplified plan against multiple defensive schemes because he is less likely to make mistakes with his decisions. Figure 10.4 shows a typical scouting form that assesses upcoming front and coverage tendencies.

Figure 10.4

All defense	Number		Attempts	Yards	Average
	49		Runs	52	204 3.9
34 strong	19		Passes	28	42 1.5
34 weak	5		Total	80	246 3.1
43 double eagle	2				
43 stack	2		Sacks	7	−32 −4.6
43 weak	1		Interceptions	1	
34 straight	1				
34 tight	1				

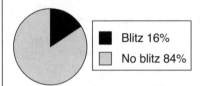

■ Blitz 16%
☐ No blitz 84%

Offensive running yards per attempt

Into strength 3.1

Away from strength 4.3

	Left	Middle	Right
Long k	0–3 -9 yards	0–0 0 yards	0–0 0 yards
Medium m	1–1 14 yards	0–0 0 yards	0–0 0 yards
Short s	1–4 3 yards	1–4 8 yards	4–16 26 yards

(continued)

Sample opponent scouting form showing an overview of the defense.

Figure 10.4 *(continued)*

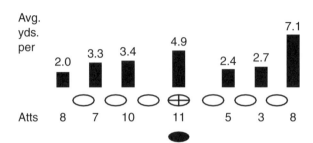

Coverage/defense	Number	Yards	Blitz
1 free	**75**	**237**	**None (64), 2 cat (3), 4 blood (1), other (1), 3 axe (1), 4 axe (1), 13 catblood (1), stab weak (1), 4 cat (1), axe cat weak (1)**
43 base	28	124	None (24), 2 cat (2), 4 blood (1), other (1)
43 stack	18	66	None (15), 2 cat (1), 3 axe (1), 4 axe (1)
34 strong	17	29	None (15), 13 catblood (1), stab weak (1)
34 weak	5	2	None (5)
43 double eagle	2	5	None (2)
34 eagle	1	14	None (1)
34 tight	1	0	4 cat (1)
43 weak	1	0	None (1)
34 straight	1	−1	None (1)
43 eagle	1	−2	Axe cat weak (1)
2	**2**	**8**	**None (2)**
43 base	2	8	None (2)
1	**2**	**1**	**13 catblood (1), other (1)**
34 strong	2	1	13 catblood (1), other (1)
2 free	**1**	**0**	**None (1)**
43 stack	1	0	None (1)

Evaluating Their Personnel

Measuring the talent level of the other team is usually easy. Statistics, reputation, studying videotapes, and scouting are tools that can be used to evaluate the players on the other team. Knowing just what the other team's players can and can't do is the basis for game planning, along with identifying their system of play. The game evaluation and individual performance form, explained in chapter 13, can be used to record information on your opponent, as well.

Elements to be considered are speed, size, athletic ability, experience, football savvy, and effectiveness in the system of play. A productive approach in evaluating these factors is to use a form when scouting or studying videotapes that allows careful scrutiny of the other team's personnel (see table 10.1).

There is nothing more critical in preparing for an opponent than a well-schooled scout team. A scout team that can duplicate what the opponent is going to execute in the upcoming game provides realistic game conditions that ultimately prepare the quarterback and team. Correct technique and high-gear tempo on the part of the scout team offer realistic repetition, which in turn has great carryover value come game time.

Making a defensive scout team work begins with making a coach responsible for the scout team's execution. Coaching the scout team (and thus the quarterback to some extent) on the opponent's defense is everything to offensive preparation. The scout team coach must possess the following characteristics to guarantee effectiveness:

- He is well versed on the opponent's system of defense.
- He has access to appropriate personnel for the team's makeup.
- He meets early with the scout team each game week and organizes their roles.
- He has play cards diagrammed with specific fronts, coverages, and blitzes.
- He spends extra time with the quarterback going over details of the opponent's scheme, such as line movement, linebacker depth, and the personalities of coverage and defensive personnel.
- He has identified contain and primary forces from each defense for the quarterback.
- He can teach the scout team front technique penetration or read.

Table 10.1 Personnel Rating Form: Opponents

Team: _____ Year: _____

Player #	Name	Position	Ability	Speed	Height	Weight	Experience

The defensive scout team's performance also should mirror the pursuit of opponents, whether it be active or nonactive. Tendencies of the defense, such as how they play on hash mark, down and distance, and at various yard lines are also important. Again, the realism of the scout team is at the heart of preparation.

Analyzing Matchups

The outcome of every contest is determined by the individual matchups: offensive linemen against defensive linemen, receivers working against defensive backs, running backs challenging linebackers. Each matchup pits the physical and mental skills of one person against another. From these exchanges, come the advantage desired—a winning edge. The team that wins most of the matchups likely will dominate the contest.

Looking for and isolating advantageous matchups in preparation for a contest is a big part of game planning. It is important to cover up weaknesses at a position matchup with the system of play or by providing help from another teammate. Speed mismatches are perhaps the most glaring of all comparisons and often most costly. Height, quickness, or experience can supply advantage to a team's arsenal of weapons.

When deciding how to use advantages, there are some considerations to explore. Establish the formation or alignment that pits the strongest, fastest guy on your team against the weakest on the other team. Use a man in motion to force the defense into a desirable matchup because coverage requires specific adjustment to the late change of offensive formation strength. Isolating and detaching a receiver or running back away from the formation strength can prevent a defense from double coverage on a particular player.

Sometimes matchups give the opposition the advantage, requiring the offense to counter. Specific formations, plays, and techniques are the solution. The quarterback has a lot to do with recognizing and efficiently operating to overcome whatever the disadvantage may be. He can call for the formation or play that most likely handicaps the defender, making the defense unable to create havoc through the mismatch. The use of a back or tight end to help block a great pass rusher is a common adjustment to counter a specific advantage.

Running the play away from the opponent's best is also a smart strategy. Trapping a defensive lineman can serve to neutralize the lineman. The draw play penalizes a great pass rusher and once again places him in a mode of uncertainty.

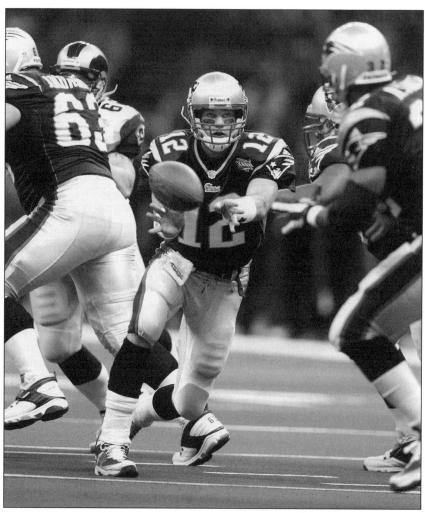

■ By scouting the defense you can isolate matchups that favor your offense. Use your offensive strengths to move the ball up the field.

There are two primary objectives in matchups: use personnel to your advantage or dilute the effectiveness of the other team's personnel. Both of these goals can be accomplished with forethought and preparation through the effective performance of a scout team.

Committing Practice Time

Substantial practice is of incredible importance for quarterback efficiency. Perfection and execution always stem from repetition. There never seems to be enough time to cover all aspects of offense, defense, and the kicking game.

Often it comes down to making choices not only about the specifics within the game plan but the potential game conditions that need to be created to adequately test and evaluate the plan. Practicing the plan on the appropriate yard line and hash is most important. Lining up the scout team correctly provides necessary realism. Add a clock to drills, and include a whistle to control the action to make the environment more gamelike. One time during game week, use officials, lights, crowd noise, game uniforms, and game communication to assist in producing a realistic atmosphere.

Meetings and studying videotapes are not a substitute for on-the-field practice but can be used to reduce the amount of verbal communication in practice sessions. Preparing for practice, setting daily goals, and emphasizing certain techniques can be covered at these off-field meetings, saving valuable field time for executing drills and running plays in gamelike situations. Table 10.2 shows a sample practice schedule for a quarterback.

Good organization and constructive drills will help conserve time, allowing for added repetitions of the game plan itself. The amount of time doesn't necessarily guarantee absorption of the plan. Good, constructive, motivational instruction is the best way to learn. What the quarterback says and how he says it affect the understanding process that will produce the desired or undesired action at game time.

Table 10.2   Quarterback Practice Schedule— Tuesday/Wednesday

Minutes	Instruction	Comments
10:00	Warm up	Jog one lap around field Stretch Play catch Throw and set up drills
5:00	Handoffs and fakes	
10:00	Throw individual routes from passing tree	
20:00	Outside drill/skeleton	Versus zone and man coverage
10:00	Red-zone and green-zone passing	Plays versus air
10:00	Situations	Versus pressure Third-down plays
10:00	Hash-mark offense	Versus pressure Wide-side plays
20:00	Team	Move the ball, get first downs Speed up and slow down offense Special plays

Visualizing and Anticipating

The game plan is always more productive when the quarterback prepares well. Good preparation will give him confidence, insight into the big picture, and details about the defense. These considerations foster a deeper understanding in the quarterback of the what, how, where, and when of the plan. Confidence comes from concentration and thought. Insight comes from intense study and active involvement in the physical assignments included in the plan.

A tactic that helps enormously is for the quarterback to visualize the aspects of the game plan he is involved in by closing his eyes and focusing his mind on assignments. The image in his mind needs to be vivid, complete with environmental details, as well as the plan itself. The closer the signal caller can get to imagining the real thing, the better!

Studying videotapes of the opponent and cutups of formations and plays against probable defensive alignments is a tremendous learning tool for the quarterback. After studying the videotapes, the quarterback and coach can make corrections to the plan, refine it, and even eliminate anything that might not work. Study videotapes early in the week so that there is time for changes to be made and practiced. Studying videotapes is an excellent tool for the quarterback to use to learn about the opponent and the skills of his own team. A quarterback can study videotapes with his coach or on his own.

Game plan specifics and practice on Monday and Tuesday should be videotaped. A Wednesday morning meeting with the team gives the coach and quarterback time to present the plan and work through adjustments. This way, the field general can grow with the plan. He can see vividly and feel the concepts. With this growth comes confidence and belief in what is to be done that weekend.

For a quarterback, studying practice videotapes is like playing the game before the contest. He can see mistakes, evaluate them, and make adjustments when necessary. This activity is comparable to shooting a gun at a target and missing, then adjusting the sights and shooting again.

Creating the Game Plan

Numerous forms can help keep track of how the game plan is going, using the game plan as the primary reference. The information on these forms ranges from general information to ongoing play-by-play accounts of the game itself. Forms that are extremely useful are

- a tip sheet that includes a list of keys from the game plan given to the quarterback the day before the game;
- a scouting report, which is a multipage, in-depth document that shows the strengths and weaknesses of the other team's personnel and scheme;
- a call sheet that provides the coaches and quarterback with situation calls and information, which is used on the field, in the press box, and often on a wristband the quarterback wears;

- an alignment form, a form used to keep track of the opposition's fronts and alignments during the game, which is used to help the quarterback select plays and make blocking calls;
- a coverage recognition sheet, a form that checks coverage during the game against formations, frequency of coverage, and adjustments to motion, which helps play selection and choice of formation or motion; and
- a halftime accounting form that compiles the information accumulated in the first half to be used for the second half.

No form is more valuable than the offensive game plan form. This is the blueprint from which game strategy and execution are drawn. Columns identifying formations and plays can be constructed a number of ways on this form. An easy method is to color code the formation and plays into first-down or second and third normal calls. For example, first-down plays may be shown in red; second down, in blue; and third down, in green.

Color coding by downs makes it easy for anyone to see and use the form during a game. Calls not in the normal range of use should be placed elsewhere on the form and labeled situation calls. Figure 10.5 shows part of a typical game script. It shows how game information is organized for play calling.

A complete game plan has many elements yet should be simple to use. A one-page alphabetical listing is the most suitable way to present information. Categories should include all the plays by formations to be used in the game. This list can be broken down into pass plays and run plays. Plays by situations should appear on the right side of the plan.

Planning for First Downs

More than anything else, the function of the quarterback is to obtain first downs. To win, a football team has to make first downs. There are few shortcuts that allow a team to succeed unless they get first downs. There are numerous approaches to getting first downs, so it is a matter of using the play that can best get the job done at that time.

Sometimes it comes down to the signal caller making the right play call in the huddle or on the line of scrimmage. In other situations, the quarterback must make a crucial decision within the play, such as whom to throw to or give the ball to on an option play.

Figure 10.5

1 & 10	#	Hash	Pers	Formation	Motion	Play	Key	
	1		Z	I RT Slot		3 Lead		
	2		T	RT WG T	H	5 Zone		
	3		R	LT TRIPS		600 thunder	W	
	4		T	RT TREY		600 Y slip screen		
	5		T	LT TRIPLES	XiN	9 TOSS		
Hash	1		R	LT TRIPS		3 Send		
	2		T	TRIPLES RT	XiN	6 Reverse		BALANCE
	3	R	Z	I RT PRO		80 Hitch		
	4		T	LT TREY T		5 Zone		
	5	R	Z	JK LT Slot	ZiN	8 TOSS Pass		
	6	R	R	RT TRIPS B		500 NUKE		
	7	R	TH	RT T		91		

SCRIPT

- I LT slot 3 lead
- RT Rey T Zh 8 TOSS
- RT TRIPS 5 Zone
- LT TRIPLES Xin 728
- RT T H 6 CTR
- RT TRIPS B 500 NUKE

Sample game script.

Regardless of how it's done, getting the first down is the main objective. A high percentage of games won will parallel the number of first downs obtained. Therefore, a good quarterback finds ways to get first downs.

To move the team 10 yards, the quarterback must

- know his offense;
- set up the defense for first-down situation plays;
- correctly use his personnel;
- use field location to his advantage;
- let the formation help with matchups that exploit the defense;
- apply motion to force the defense to change alignments;
- get the ball in the hands of the best player;
- call plays proved to get the job done; and
- avoid overusing plays that are high risk, such as double handoffs, gadget plays, or slow-developing plays.

He must always carefully analyze the down-and-distance situation when determining what to do to get the first down. What the offense can and can't do is influenced by down and distance. Though in theory, every play is designed to score, the reality is that the defense is going to get in the way. It is important to build into the offensive plan what the defense is likely to do in a given situation. The field general's responsibility is to sort through all the possibilities so that the play has a greater opportunity to succeed. Those 10 yards can seem like a mile but only to those who think that way. When a quarterback has a plan and knows the plan, he then is capable of executing the plan.

CHAPTER 11

GAME MANAGEMENT

Game management begins with the kickoff and ends when the final gun sounds. What happens during this period gives every contest its direction and personality. Controlling and influencing the happenings during this 48 or 60 minutes is game management.

A quarterback always performs as if on a mission, and his contribution is monumental. Nothing is more important, however, than how the quarterback manages the game. Manipulating the offense on the field is the quarterback's job. No one, other than the coach, can affect the outcome more than the quarterback.

The quarterback starts every play, by way of a silent count, foot movement, or just going when the ball is snapped. Although these methods of starting a play are less common than the traditional cadence, they nonetheless have a place in today's game. Many factors influence the method a team uses to start play. The quarterback is the key regardless of the system.

For a silent count, the quarterback starts the count with a word or hand signal. Then the team picks up the cadence and counts silently. Currently, this approach is seldom used, but in the days of Knute Rockne it was a popular system. Overcoming crowd noise is generally the reason for using silent cadence today.

Foot movement is commonly used for a detached receiver off the line of scrimmage who can't see the football move or hear the cadence. The quarterback simply picks up his heel when the ball is to be snapped. This snap count approach can be used whether the quarterback is under the center or in shotgun position.

Going when the ball is snapped rather than on cadence is a technique employed by detached receivers or when a back is in motion facing the ball. The quarterback just calls the signal, and these players if they can't hear release upfield when the football comes up.

Victory Comes From Good Decisions

I was the head coach at the University of Montana. In 1995, during the national championship game against Marshall University, my quarterback, Dave Dickenson, exhibited good game-winning judgment. During our final drive on a third and goal, Dave threw the football into the ground when the receiver was covered instead of trying to force a completion, which allowed us to kick the game-winning field goal the next play. When asked about the play, Dave said, "Coach, their cornerback was attached to our receiver, Matt Wells." His judgment was correct, and we won that important contest, thanks to his perception and wise decision.

The signal caller's leadership, experience, preparation, poise, and competitiveness tend to show up during a game and are instrumental in game management. Some quarterbacks are better than others at guiding a team through good times or crisis after crisis. Because there is no precise formula or method of managing, a quarterback has to draw from his personal assets and readiness to make things happen.

Where game management differs from other elements of quarterbacking is that the opposition and personal performance attract less focus. The primary mission for the field general is to generate, maintain, and overcome on-the-field hazards, both routine hazards and those unique to each game. The following should be the quarterback's concerns during the game:

- Get first downs.
- Don't turn over the ball.
- Take advantage of personnel.
- Manage the clock.
- Mix up the cadence.

- Avoid sacks.
- Make timely plays.
- Keep morale and enthusiasm alive.
- Communicate effectively with teammates.
- Keep good discipline in the huddle.
- Share thoughts with the coaches on the sideline.
- Handle crowd noise.

For a quarterback, managing a game is a four-quarter deal. Game tempo and knowledge of the opponent's personnel and strategy are learned on an "as you go" basis. A signal caller should get a feel for the what, how, when, and where as the game progresses. The quarterback should accomplish all the things he is not supposed to be capable of doing and do so as if it's normal!

There are other aspects of quarterbacking during a contest: making sight adjustments when needed, changing plays on the line of scrimmage, anticipating blitz and coverage, communicating with the referee as appropriate, conferring about strategy between plays and on the sideline, and directing and correcting the receiver splits to the advantage of each play.

Because offensive plays generally begin in the huddle, a more in-depth analysis of the huddle is covered in the next section. The importance of the huddle can't be stressed enough. Momentum for every play begins in the huddle.

The Huddle

A truly outstanding coach in the 1960s was Oregon State's Dee Andros. At a clinic in 1966, Coach Andros wisely said, "Most good things that happen offensively begin in the huddle." Much like a commander in the field, the quarterback has to be on top of all aspects of the huddle. The design and focus of the huddle and the communication in it are the responsibility of the quarterback and no one else. He is in charge of the huddle from beginning to end.

Because the purpose of the huddle is to supply information about to be put into action, everyone in the huddle must concentrate. This focus begins as the huddle is about to come together. In other words, there should be no discussion or talk of any kind, except that of the signal caller during the entire preparation time for the execution of the play to come.

The other 10 players need to hear correctly what the quarterback says, or a mental or physical mistake will likely occur. Calls break down into formation/play/motion/starting count. Ideally, the formation and play should be repeated twice in the call. A typical call would be "right trips," describing a formation; "24 dive," naming the play; and the words "on two," stating the cadence. In the huddle, the quarterback would say, "Right trips, 24 dive, on two," pause for one second, then repeat the call.

Following the call, the huddle breaks with a word or phrase that releases the players to the line of scrimmage. Normally words such as "ready, break" or "ready, go" are used to release players from the huddle. All this comprises huddle procedure. Any questions or other information between players and quarterback occurs before the huddle convenes or after it breaks.

There are some essential characteristics of a well-managed huddle beyond the calling of the play. Proper alignment of the huddle, stance of participants, and method of departure from the huddle are significant to the overall discipline needed for best execution. Eye contact with players, hand placement of players, and focused concentration are major objectives.

Huddles can be shaped a variety of acceptable ways. A circle open to the line of scrimmage or with backs to the football is most common. What is important is that there is a procedure and that it is conducive to order and efficiency. Players can stand upright or kneel, as long as all players assume the same predetermined posture. The huddle must be organized so that all players can see and hear the calls but also allow for easy release to the line of scrimmage. For example, in an open huddle (figure 11.1a) or one in which the players' backs are to the line of scrimmage, linemen should make up the front line closest to the football, with wide receivers in the second line and on the outside edge. Running backs are in the middle of the back line. For the quarterback, what is most critical is that each player can see his mouth and is close enough to hear instructions.

The circle huddle (figure 11.1b) had its origin in early football but still has many advantages. The most important advantage is that unity comes within a circle and focus is forced on the call. The advantages of the open-faced huddle is that the quarterback can see the defensive personnel and the open-faced huddle prevents the players in the huddle from being distracted by the defense.

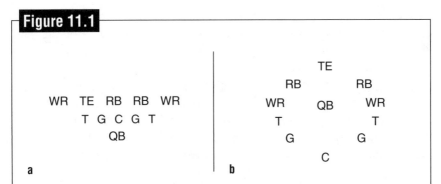

Figure 11.1

Huddle formations. (*a*) In the open-faced huddle, the QB's back is to the LOS. (*b*) In the circle huddle, the QB is in the middle.

Regardless of the huddle alignment used, the quarterback should position himself near the huddle while it is being formed and in line to see the opposition and his coaches on the sideline.

When calling the play, the quarterback's voice has to be clear and loud enough for his teammates to hear. Good enunciation helps players read his lips. He turns his head slowly back and forth so that all players can see and hear the call. The quarterback should repeat the call twice.

Releasing the team from the huddle is important not only for quick positioning on the line of scrimmage but also to generate an enthusiastic mind-set. Clapping of hands and brisk movement to the line help reinforce confidence and a positive feeling for the execution of the play. Getting to the line of scrimmage quickly also provides additional time for the quarterback to have on the ball. He should lead the huddle break and clap with a vigorous "ready, break."

Communication With Coaches and Teammates

Good communication is vital in football to disseminate needed information. All communication goes in two directions—between the quarterback and the other players and between the quarterback and the coaches. This information highway is the basis for common understanding and execution. A team cannot function effectively without adequate communication.

The most common type of communication a quarterback uses is verbal, but written communication and body language also serve vital roles in communication exchanges.

Each communication method has a specific purpose. Pertinent thoughts, instruction, on-the-spot corrections, play calling, phone exchanges, and position insights are normal verbal communications that occur in every contest (see table 11.1). Written communication includes keeping track of statistical data, usually on forms, and noting game information before the contest (see chapter 10).

A Case of Quarterback Confidence

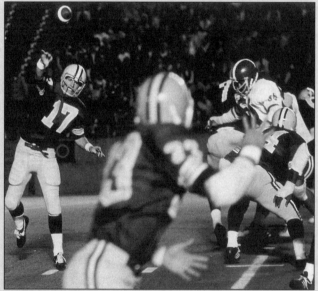

Courtesy of Don Read

With only seconds remaining in a crucial game, Norv Turner, my quarterback at the University of Oregon, said, "Go for it," on fourth down and a yard. We were behind by three points, and I was thinking field goal. Norv's confidence and determination influenced our decision, and he crossed the goal line seconds later on a keeper, winning the game for us. Once again, a quarterback's insightfulness and competitive desire led to a huge win.

Table 11.1 Accumulative Ongoing Game Data

Down and distance	Hash	Formation	Play	Front	Stunt	Cover	Gain

Clock Management

For the quarterback, clock management falls into two distinct areas: the 30-second clock (time allowed between plays) and the running clock that tracks the overall game time. Good management means using both of these clocks to the team's advantage. Quarterbacks have to understand how the rules of the game affect the clock.

Whether a team runs the football or passes it can seem to lengthen or shorten the contest. Because running plays take more time to execute, the flow of a game can be influenced by running the ball. On the other hand, a game is lengthened by increasing the ratio of passes thrown. Remember, the clock stops when the football hits the ground, as with an incomplete pass. This means the clock doesn't start again until the center snaps the ball. Contrast this with a running play that stays in bounds when there is no first down achieved—the clock continues to run (in college football rules). An injury or time-out will stop the clock.

A quarterback can increase or decrease the number of plays in a game by simply running or passing more. The nature of the plays, pass or run, affect the running time and game clock.

The quarterback can do even more to control the time in a game by influencing the tempo of his offense. Keeping the team in the huddle or on the line of scrimmage for the maximum time allowed can burn a lot of seconds off the clock. If he uses only 7 to 10 seconds (more or less) between plays, the quarterback can allow as many as 10 to 12 additional plays. If he uses the full allotted time (25 or 30 seconds, depending on the level of competition), the quarterback can reduce the number of plays.

The score, momentum, time left on the clock, injuries, weather conditions, and other factors generally contribute to a team's clock strategy. But whether the team is hanging on to a lead, catching up, or controlling the entire game, clock management is of paramount importance to winning. The signal caller's judgment, foresight, and instincts must be keen. He must know the rules and the game plan, and the opponent's personnel and strategy. The quarterback also can draw from game psychology and philosophy. Injuries may also determine how the quarterback manages the clock. These factors can add minutes to the game or take them away.

Communication from the sideline to the quarterback is influencial in determining strategy. Hand signals and player substitutions make up an important relay system. Wristbands (figure 11.2) worn by

Figure 11.2

A wristband can help a quarterback quickly determine the best play.

the quarterback, and sometimes others on the team, can be helpful. Time between plays is still another opportunity for additional communication.

Two-Minute Offense

Clock management is truly put to the test when running a two-minute drill. Doug Flutie, John Elway, and Dan Fouts come to mind when you look at how to conserve time and move the football. Through their leadership and perception of opponents' alignment and coverage, these greats made the most of limited time on the clock. They managed time-outs, stopped the clock when necessary, and controlled their teammates.

In a two-minute situation, the quarterback has to have a handle on when and where on the field to call the predetermined plays. Usually, formations are reduced to one or two types for simplicity. Motion is normally eliminated, and the cadence is always on one or first sound after the set is called. Hash-mark position can also influence play selection, as some plays need the room provided when located in the middle of the field or into the wide side.

There are five factors that stop the clock: throwing an incomplete pass, downing the ball, calling a time-out, marking off a penalty, or when a player gets injured. A quarterback has control over three—the incomplete pass, downing the football, and calling a time-out. When to use any of the three depends on the game plan, the coach's direction, and the quarterback's judgment.

To ensure good communication between the quarterback and the sideline, the field general must look to the sideline between every play. He should position himself between the huddle and sideline (or between the formation and sideline if the huddle is not used) to hear and see the coach supplying the information. When the quarterback is unable to position himself optimally because of the ball in play, he must draw from his preparation, expertise, and knowledge. This situation proves that wristbands are great resources for a quarterback.

When operating a two-minute offense, the quarterback also must communicate with the referee as to when a time-out will be called. As soon as the play ends, the quarterback must call one of two things—"huddle, huddle" or "on the ball, on the ball." While the team is getting ready, the quarterback receives information from the sideline or gets under the center to start the next play.

Good pass plays for a two-minute offense are outs, corner routes, fades, and hitches. If a time-out is available, you can use combination patterns. Layer combinations provide the quarterback with choices for throwing the ball. Crossing patterns are also effective combinations. Even some carefully selected running plays can help, as long as there is a time-out to use.

One final consideration for the field general is to be aware that coverage normally differs from what a defense employs the other 46 or 58 minutes of the game. In both high school and college football, the two minutes before halftime and the final two minutes of a game often signal a change in philosophy for both the offense and defense.

Defenses usually place one or two more defensive backs into the game to strengthen coverage. From the quarterback's point of view, this fact changes pattern selection and timing of some plays. The quarterback will be working with a reduced number of plays that can be effective. Keying may change as a result of the nickel or dime (five or six defensive backs) packages. Receivers, too, may need to adjust routes to accomplish the desired mission. On the positive side, a quarterback should have more time to throw the ball, as fewer linemen are involved in the rush.

Sideline Communication

A lot of communication takes place with the people on the sideline during a game. The quarterback has access to every player and every coach, and via field phones, the press box staff. For this reason, the players on the sideline must be grouped by position for easy location.

A quarterback should follow this sequence of stations between each offensive series. As soon as he leaves the field, he needs to check with the appropriate coach—the head coach, offensive coordinator, or quarterback coach. Next, he checks in with either the offensive line or receivers, depending on what input he needs. If he needs to converse with the press box, the order of stops may change. If time allows, the quarterback can drink water, get off his feet, or review the game plan. If an ongoing opponent coverages and fronts form (as shown in figure 13.1, page 254) is kept, he can review and absorb this data. On the professional level, end zone and sometimes side-view still photos of coverages and fronts are available.

Wristbands are an extremely useful form of communication. An entire game plan or just selected plays can be stored on a wristband. In a no-huddle offense, the entire offense can wear wristbands to identify the play being called. Sometimes, just the detached receivers who have a hard time hearing audibles use wristbands. A wristband should include play numbers, formations, and plays. Cadence for the play can also be put on the band if a particular count goes with the play. Bold typing or underlining can be used to highlight certain plays.

Laminating the band will prevent deterioration from sweat or rain. A right-handed player should put the band on his left wrist; a left-handed player should put it on his right wrist. It is also possible to use two wristbands, with running plays on one and passing plays on the other. Sometimes the information on wristbands is revised or changed at halftime to eliminate or emphasize plays.

Management looms big among the quarterback's duties. His skills are magnified for good or bad in this aspect of the game. The effect he has on a contest in this facet of his job is enormous and often taken for granted. The quarterback makes more pertinent decisions while leading his team in this nonplay phase of his duties than he does in the actual running of a play. He has to be on top of what might be defined as the loose ends within the game, things that can't be handled by anyone else. In a broad sense, the quarterback acts like both an official and a coach to his team. He interprets, accumulates, advises, and directs those on the field with him. At no time in a contest does a quarterback need to be more in charge and decisive in his actions than when actively trying to regulate his team.

All quarterbacks are different in physical attributes and mental makeup. There is no absolute model for a quarterback's managing tactics, only a framework from which to function. Booker T. Washington provided a pearl of wisdom when he said, "Excellence is doing a common thing in an uncommon way." Mr. Washington's point hits at the heart of a quarterback's role in managing a game. A quarterback has his own unique style of getting the job done. What's most critical is the outcome, not the approach, when it comes to directing a team.

© Newsport Photography

▪ A good quarterback knows how to get the most out of his teammates and himself.

Take with you this important fact: The quarterback doesn't have to be big, physical, fast, or have phenomenal ability to be a good manager. What the quarterback must have is leadership, poise, and a well-thought-out plan to handle any situations that might occur. Game management means attention to details, anticipating and regulating those activities that confront a team during the contest itself. Good game management means overcoming the obstacles encountered, with the assets available, and making maximal use of people at the right time and in the right setting.

A good manager hears all, sees all, and knows all. Not an easy job for the field general on game day! That's why he makes the big bucks, as they say in professional football. If a quarterback doesn't manage well, he better be a superstar player to compensate. Management in this era requires both directing and producing. It means evaluating and motivating, as well as performing. Maybe more than anything else, managing comes down to coordinating so that others can do what they do best. There can be only one manager on the field, and that guy is the quarterback. He is the final word, the trigger man for every offense and, for that matter, every team.

Management is more than performing. Any quarterback can contribute personally with his physical talents, but a great quarterback does more. The influence the field general has on others best measures his worth.

What makes a quarterback special in the area of game management? How does the team function, from the kickoff until the final gun? The quarterback's ability to operate within the framework of each game is only part of the quarterback's challenge. He is expected to make decisions that influence the direction of the game. A quarterback must rise above all situations.

Few contests are won with poor management, though many games are won with good management. When the game is over and accountability sets in, the media (among others) always ask the quarterback the "why" questions: Why did you call this play, why didn't you do that? So it is in the life of a quarterback.

CHAPTER 12

COMMUNICATION AND TERMINOLOGY

In the football world, there is a language common to the game itself. These are the words, terms, and phrases used to disseminate and interpret information during the game. Terminology in a football program serves to link players and production, so it is of critical importance to whatever is accomplished by a team. The precise use of words allows one person in a football operation to communicate with another. To keep everyone on the same page is the primary function of terminology. Without this special language, there would be havoc and confusion. Football terminology provides the basis for all understanding of commonly used information. The depth and breadth of these words are the life support to a team, as the veins and blood vessels are to the human body.

Football terminology is unique and ever changing because of rule modifications, natural evolution, and modern technology. Words command, signal, or express messages among participants. These words and phrases are used on the field to prompt thought or action.

The quarterback must be sensitive to rule changes and innovations and absorb their full meaning. A dictionary of football terms published just a few years ago would list maybe half the words used today to describe action. As the game gets more and more specialized, the quarterback will be increasingly challenged to stay abreast of new words and changing meanings.

Within this vocabulary is a separate grouping of terms an offense uses. To perform effectively, the quarterback should have complete perception of these many words. Terminology can be classified into several categories for a quarterback.

Because each position on a team uses its own terminology, it is imperative that the field general have a full grasp of the words for each of these positions. In addition, a signal caller will supply information to and receive information from his coaches and teammates. Terminology is a tool used to explain or identify. Correct terminology leads to clear communication and good results. Improper use of words slows the transmission of information and handicaps those committed to the task at hand. For this reason, any functional offensive playbook should include a section on terminology.

Every football program uses some terminology unique to its own style. The most commonly used words define all facets of quarterback play that deal with technique, methodology, and philosophy. These special words act to clarify the how, when, where, and why of offensive football.

Few other things in football can play havoc with execution as misuse or misunderstanding of terminology can. Although each team has its own way of using words, most football terminology transcends team lines. The challenge for a quarterback is to establish a thorough understanding of the football jargon he uses with those who make up the offense.

Quarterback duties are far-reaching. The quarterback is obviously the coach on the field. He is the team's manager of all offensive

Courtesy of Don Read

▪ Quarterback communication is essential to success.

output. As the offensive game has widened in scope, so has the volume of terminology to provide necessary communication.

Winston Churchill once said, "I am always ready to listen; it's the learning I hate." For a quarterback, learning means everything to his ability to function. He must understand all football terminology or risk offensive ineffectiveness. He limits his team's productivity if he cannot appropriately use the terms or words he needs to.

When everyone is on the same page, good things have a better chance of happening. An Irish proverb says that even a small thorn can cause great pain. When the quarterback and others interpret words in the same manner, there is a meaningful connection that allows input without hesitation. He can operate quickly and efficiently, which should be his goal all the time. Today's sophisticated game demands descriptive terms to describe the inner working of all components.

A close examination of a football program reveals that there are numerous cores of vocabulary within the whole. The breakdown extends from individual positions to units such as offense, defense, special teams, scouting, and administration. A quarterback needs to have a handle on much of this specialized terminology for quality operational execution. Like the coach, he is involved in one way or another with the use of a wide range of football terminology as he directs those he is responsible to and for.

The quarterback is simply more effective when he is in sync with all of a team's spoken and written exchanges. Every member of the offense must be on the same wavelength. Terminology is the foundation for understanding the rudiments of offensive football. In the most basic analysis, communication and terminology are the nuts and bolts of offensive football. The quarterback is the primary vehicle of communication to those who perform in a game. Without correct terminology, there will be little understanding. Terms simplify knowledge and explain through language information necessary for creating appropriate action.

The quarterback not only speaks to those he is responsible for but also for these same people. More than that, he listens to the players he directs for advice and reaction to his commands. This process is communication in its most vivid form. A quarterback is more effective at informing when he is able to assemble a meaningful vocabulary of terms that is of particular worth to each element of offensive football. Following is a list of these terms.

alley—Place between the defensive corner and the safety.

alley oop—High-trajectory pass thrown in the end zone where the receiver catches it at the highest point.

angle—Shortest line to the ball from any route or pattern.

arrow route—Route at about a 30-degree angle to the sideline, normally used by tight ends, running backs, or slots.

back side—Area of play away from the point of attack; routes run that are secondary to the on-side pattern or route.

bail—Technique that corners use to drop back quickly in zone coverage.

ball control—Hold onto the football for long periods of time.

ball position—Position between football and defender.

ball securement—Covering both points of the football and keeping it against the body.

banana—Route where receiver releases outside then bends inward.

banjo—Used in man coverage when two receivers are within five yards of each other.

base count—Method used to determine who blocks whom; the count of defensive linemen is from inside out.

basics—Plays that do not require elaborate execution; established foundation of a system.

big play—Any play that shifts the momentum of a game, provides a first down or touchdown, or gets the team out of poor field position.

blue area—Area on the field between the +45- to the +20-yard lines.

body tilt—Angle that the running back assumes while carrying the football; demonstrates his weight distribution.

bracket—Defenders switch coverage on receivers within their coverage responsibility; can be used against deep or shallow routes.

broken I—Football off set behind guard or tackle; back in normal I depth.

bucket step—Lineman's short step back and to the play side.

bump and run—Tight, aggressive man-to-man cover with defender playing an inside-out technique.

bunch—Formation that groups three receivers close together.

center of gravity—Running back's weight distribution to determine balance.

cheat—Change the running back's alignment to aid execution of the play.

check—Change of assignment or play usually done on the line of scrimmage; a mental and physical pause to determine if a linebacker is blitzing before executing assignment.

chip technique—Blocking a defender's shoulder or hip, then moving on to another defender.

chop—Block on a defensive player below the waist; usually used by tackles.

combo routes—Two or more routes used together to break down coverage and open one receiver.

comeback—Relationship a receiver needs to assume to the quarterback; squared-up receiver moving back to the quarterback.

confront—To take on a specific defensive alignment.

corner route—To the back of the end zone where the sideline and back line meet; the ball is thrown to this spot and the receiver catches it high and over his shoulder.

cover 1—Man-to-man coverage with a free safety.

cover 2—Corners roll in outside shade position playing short zone; two deep safeties cover half the field each.

cover 3—Three-deep zone with strong safety rotated to formation strength.

cover 4—Man-to-man coverage without a free safety.

cover 5—Also referred to as *nickel coverage*, where an extra defensive back is used.

cover 6—Use of a linebacker or extra strong safety in deep cover.

cover 7—Combo cover zone with a four-man rush.

cover 8—Combo cover zone with a three-man rush.

crack—Block from split position inside on a defender, attacking a linebacker, safety, or defensive end.

cross—Deeper route receivers use behind linebacker depth across the middle of the field.

crossover step—Bring one foot over the other foot on the first step, usually a short step; used by a quarterback on his drop.

crowd the ball—Offensive linemen line up as close to the football as possible without being offside.

curl—Route in which the receiver stops, squares up, and sinks inside; ranges in depth from 12 to 15 yards.

cushion—Distance between players or between a receiver and the defensive backs; may vary from one to three yards.

cut back—Quarterback's path changes from one direction to another to beat pursuit.

cutoff—Step to the gap to prevent the penetration of a defensive lineman.

delay—Pass play that does not begin until the under cover has dropped; there is about two seconds of delay before the pattern develops.

dig—Cross route from one side of the formation to the other.

disguise—Defense hides its intended coverage through its initial alignment.

double cover—Two secondary defenders cover one receiver; can be from a man or zone cover package.

down blocking—Stepping with the inside foot and blocking inside to wall off the defender.

downhill—Fourth quarter; used as a form of positive psychology.

down the pipe—Middle of the playing field.

drag—Shallow receiver route at linebacker depth or shorter across the middle third of the field; no more than 10 yards deep.

drive—Series of plays.

drive block—Block used to create upfield movement on a defender.

drop—Position and depth of a secondary player; usually connected to zone cover.

eagle shade—Tackles shade inside; usually used in 50 front defense.

east/west—From sideline to sideline.

end over—Put both ends on the same side of the formation, normally the wide side of the field.

exchange block—Two offensive linemen switch assignments; sometimes referred to as a *cross block.*

exchange point—Place where the quarterback and running back meet and the quarterback hands the ball off to the running back.

field position—Area of the field where the offense begins its drive.

fill—Block a hole left by a pulling offensive lineman; a running back usually fills.

firm pass pro—Protection with the objective of blocking along the front without giving ground; used when throwing short or intermediate passes.

first sound—Ball is snapped on the first word barked by the quarterback after the team has set for one second.

flair control—Running back flows to one side or the other to influence the linebackers' coverage.

flash influence—Show pass pro quickly and go to assigned block on linebacker or safety.

flood—Two or more receivers in one zone; almost always flood patterns are run in the outside third of the field.

flow—Direction of pursuit or coverage; almost always flow will be to the football.

fly—Same as fade vertical route deep, well outside release.

fold blocking—Block that brings an offensive lineman up inside the next offensive lineman; can be a tackle inside guard or guard around center.

football position—Knees-bent, buttocks-down position assumed before contact or in a head-up movement of backs and receivers on defenders.

four-down area—Area on the field when a punt on fourth down is not likely to occur; between +40 yards and opponent's goal line.

framework of the offense—Center, guards, and tackles; also called *interior line.*

get off—Accelerate from stance on count to drive block normally.

go—Upfield vertical route.

go-to guy—Receiver the quarterback is most likely to throw to because of the receiver's proved ability.

green area—Area of the field from the team's own goal line to the –20-yard line.

G scheme—Onside guard pulls and leads or traps.

half field—Safeties' responsibility; two-deep tactic used mostly in zone coverage.

hard count—Quarterback changes his voice pitch and head movement in an attempt to draw the defense offside.

H back—Blocker, fullback, or tight end used by most teams in short-yardage situations.

help—Call another lineman to help double block a defender.

high point—Where the receiver and ball meet when the football flight begins descent.

hitch—Stop route that receivers use versus zone cover, usually run 5 to 10 yards.

hot—Receiver or back who needs to look for the football immediately after the snap because the quarterback faces a linebacker, usually unblocked, and must get rid of the ball.

hurry up "O"—Attempt by the offense to get more plays run; see **lengthen the game.**

impact—Player or strategy that changes the circumstances in a game.

influence direction—Lineman moves in a direction away from the hole being run, setting up the defender to be blocked by someone else.

intermediate routes—Receiver runs behind linebacker drops and in front of deep coverage, about 13 to 20 yards deep.

into the boundary—Area from the near hash mark to the sideline; in high school football, it means one-third of the field.

iso—Play designed to attack a designated defender with a back leading on the linebacker.

keying—Quarterback looks at a defensive secondary player to determine where to throw the ball and to whom.

kick—Inside-out, chest-high block, usually used on a contain defender.

kick step—First step of an offensive tackle blocking a wide rush; short drop step with angle of interception to rusher.

kill the clock—Quarterback throws the ball into the ground to stop the clock.

lead—One running back goes in front of another to the hole or in front of the play; used mostly on sweeps and iso plays.

lead play—Most featured or used play in an offense.

lengthen the game—Use legal methods to stop the clock and gain more chances to make plays; strategies include getting out of bounds, moving in and out of the huddle quickly, throwing the football more than running it, and using time-outs.

live color—Part of the quarterback's call on the line of scrimmage; when the live color is called, it triggers a change from the called play.

lock—Form of man-to-man cover with all defensive backs assigned to someone.

log—Block outside leg of defender; normally used by pulling guard on defender.

long count—Holding or lengthening the count beyond the normal count; often used in an attempt to draw the defense offside.

long trap—Trapping the last defender on the line of scrimmage; normally done by the off or back-side guard.

look ball in—Eye focus on point of football until it meets the hands.

LOS—Line of scrimmage.

make the play—Get the job done.

man protection—Pass protect blocking with assigned defenders to be blocked.

matchups—Head-to-head battles within a game between specific players; an offense can shift its players to create more desired matchups by countering strong defenders with strong offensive personnel.

milk the clock—Take as much time as allowed to run each play.

move the pile—Running back hits the line of scrimmage at maximum speed and delivers sustained contact to the opposition, getting under the defensive players' shoulder pads and driving them upfield.

moving pocket—Quarterback protection for a half roll or waggle action pass.

near foot technique—Used as first step on most blocks or pull leads.

net—Receiver's finger position on the front end of the football when catching it.

neutral zone—Area from one tip of the football to the other, extending to the sideline along the length of the football on the line of scrimmage before the snap; neither the offense nor the defense can invade the neutral zone until after the snap.

no huddle—Set at the line of scrimmage without a huddle and execute a speed-up offense.

north/south—From goal line to goal line.

off set—Same as broken I; the fullback sets behind the guard to one side or another.

over strong—When the defensive front is shifted to the strong side.

over the top—Running back leaves his feet and goes over the linemen; used in short-yardage and goal line situations.

pass action—Direction of throw.

pass off rusher—Blocking defensive lineman temporarily and then giving him to someone else to block.

pass pro—Type of pass protection used on any given pass.

peel—Lead blocker moves to the inside and blocks while leading the play upfield.

penetration—When the defense pushes through the offensive line in an attempt to get the quarterback or disrupt the play.

perimeter—Edge of the offensive formation.

pick—Two receivers working together against man coverage to cut off the defender.

picking up the blitz—Running back steps up to block a blitzing linebacker.

pitch—Live, underhand pass.

plant—Pushing off of one foot.

plug linebacker—Linebacker who steps up and comes through a gap, assigned or unassigned.

pocket protection—Pass protection around the quarterback's throwing position, usually man.

point of attack—Area or player the play is directed to; a hole in the defense toward which the play is directed.

post—Route with a stem of six to eight yards and cut to goalpost; also a block used by one offensive lineman using a drive technique while a teammate squares up and helps drive the defender upfield.

press coverage—Corner jams on the detached receiver on or near the line of scrimmage.

prestance—Two-point position used before getting into the three-point football position.

protect ball—Cover the ball with the fingers over the point and the ball in the armpit, with one forearm over the ball.

pull—Player moves from formation alignment behind the line of scrimmage to his designated place.

push concept—Entire line gets movement on the defensive line; get off.

quarterback drop—How the quarterback pulls away from the center; this drop can be one, three, five, or seven steps.

quick screen—Pass in which there is no delay in the quarterback's throw.

reach technique—Blocking to the outside gap, stepping first with the near foot to the outside.

reading—Quarterback looks to an area or group of secondary defenders to decide where to throw the ball.

read trap—Running back runs as close as possible to the buttocks of the man trapping.

red area—Area on the field from the +20-yard line to the opponent's goal line.

regroup—Come together to unite the team and focus on the plan of action.

roll-up corner—Zone cover with one or both corners rolling up in the face of the receiver.

route relationship—Distance between receivers and the sideline or defender.

rub—Receiver brushes in front of a secondary player to allow another receiver to get open.

run around—Technique used to push pass rushers beyond the quarterback.

running with authority—Being physical and hard to tackle, keeping legs moving and using high knee action.

safety valve—Going to a predetermined place and waiting for a pass; usually a running back route.

scoop block—Step with the onside foot to the defender and block him on the way to cutting off the linebacker; normally involves the guard and center.

scramble block—Block on all fours at the legs of the defender while moving arms and legs into cutoff position of defender.

scraping linebacker—Linebacker flows to play via quickest route, penetrating B or C gaps.

seal—Maintain a position between the defender and football; usually used by linemen when play goes outside.

seam—Vertical lane between defenders; usually used versus zone coverage.

secure—Block assignment before continuing on to a secondary assignment.

separation—Distance between the defender and receiver; term normally used against man cover.

settle—Sink into a hole in coverage, stop and square up, always from the outside in.

shifting the ball—Moving the football from one arm to the other, usually away from the defender.

short arm—Quarterback does not follow through with his delivery; usually happens when he does not step up to throw.

shorten the game—Use as much time as possible to run down the clock, limiting the number of plays that can be made.

short field—In the defense's territory on the plus side of the 50-yard line.

short step—Normally used by the guard on his first or last step of a block.

short trap—Crossing over one offensive position to trap a defender.

shoulders square—Body position in which the shoulders are parallel to the line of scrimmage (for example, the position the running back takes when carrying the football or blocking).

sight adjustment—Receiver and quarterback work together with signals to take advantage of the alignment of a defensive back.

sink—Receiver stays wide and slides back to the quarterback.

sky—Receiver goes up for the football; usually used in the back of the end zone.

slant—Outside receiver's route directly to the inside; quarterback can throw the ball quicker.

slide—Quarterback action that refers to his movement from the setup position; technique receivers use after hooking or curling to the inside or outside.

slide protection—Offensive linemen block in the same predetermined direction.

slotback—Running back or receiver lines up inside the widest receiver and at least a yard deep.

slow play—Strategy used to run time off the clock (for example, the offensive back carries, then stays on the ground after being tackled until he has to get up).

soft pass pro—Giving ground in exchange for time during pass protection; used with longer pass plays.

speed cut—Technique used when the defender is playing soft; a rounded corner cut.

speed-up offense—Getting the team in and out of the huddle and getting the play off as quickly as possible; strategy for conserving time on the clock.

spill—Quarterback has to run out of the pocket because of a breakdown in protection.

split adjustment—Spaces between guards and the tackle and center and guard.

spread formations—Two or more detached receivers are placed on opposite sides to widen the field.

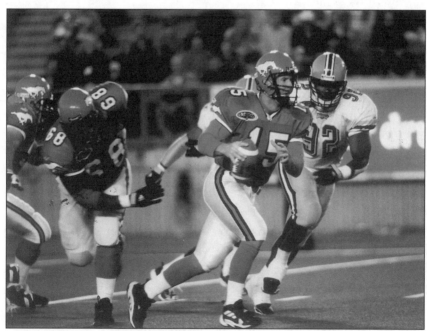

Courtesy of Don Read

■ Dave Dickenson, quarterback at the University of Montana, spills out of the pocket and scrambles away from the trailing defenders.

stack—Two or three receivers line up in tandem, normally detached from the primary formation.

stack alignment—Defensively, when linebackers set up behind guards or tackles; offensively, when one receiver sets up behind another.

step up—Quarterback moves forward into a passing lane to throw the ball; also used by the quarterback to get inside or outside the pass rushers.

stock block—Stand-up block used in the open field; body position on the defensive back is the receiver's primary objective.

stop—Timing pass route in which the receiver stops and turns inside or out and looks for the fullback.

stop route—Running back runs out of the backfield to the sideline, stops and faces the quarterback.

straight—Normal alignment.

stretch field—Strategy that allows additional room for the play to be run.

stretch horizontally—Route that widens the coverage toward the sideline.

stretch vertically—Depth of the receivers provides more space between them and the line of scrimmage toward the goal line.

strong alignment—Defensive linemen overshift to offensive strong side.

submarine—Low knee block used in short yardage and on goal line, firing out with extremely low profile and getting under opponent's shoulder pads.

surge—Offensive line comes off the ball and creates upfield movement.

swap—Two receivers switch routes; used to defeat a specific coverage.

swim move—Technique used to get by a defender; normally wide receiver against corner.

swing—Pass route usually run by a running back to one side behind the line of scrimmage.

switch ball—Move the football from one hand and arm to the other.

sync—Blend plays to produce the best results.

system—Compilation of several plays.

take it to them—Get in and out of the huddle and be aggressive.

target—Best place on a defender to make initial contact when blocking; normally shoulder to a number or to hip of defender.

tempo—Pace or rhythm of the team's performance; can be fast or slow.

third-down area—Area on the field when punting is likely on fourth down if a first down is not made; between own goal and +40-yard line.

throttle down—Slow a receiver; used between zones to get in holes of coverage.

thrust—Run through a defender, accelerating at contact point.

time of possession—Amount of time an offense has the ball during a game.

toss—Dead, two-handed flip.

to the field—Going to the wide side, from the placement of the football to the sideline.

track—Line or path a running back takes to the exchange point.

trail technique—Used by defensive backs in man cover; normally one yard inside and one yard behind the receiver.

trey block—Two linemen block two defenders, but two block one first; then one lineman comes off and blocks a second.

trips—Three detached receivers are placed to a given side of the formation.

turn back—When the entire offensive line drops outside and blocks the first man away from the play.

turnover—Offense loses the football to the defense because of an interception or fumble.

twins—Two detached receivers are split to the same side of the formation.

twist line variation—Two defensive linemen switch alignments on the move.

two-minute drill—When the offense is attempting to score in the two minutes just before halftime or at the end of the game; strategies include operating without a huddle and focusing on passes instead of runs.

unbalance—Place more offensive linemen on one side of the ball than the other in initial formation.

under cover—Area in front of the linebacker and secondary.

use the clock—Quarterback takes as much time as possible to get plays off; strategy for running time off the clock.

waggle action—Quarterback moves in one direction and changes to another; used on run or pass plays.

wall—Position block high, keeping the body between the ball and the defender.

weak alignment—Defensive linemen overshift to the offensive weak side.

wedge technique—Step with inside foot and drive block area to inside upfield.

wheel—Route that allows an inside receiver to run out and up.

wheel technique—Block made after lineman checks on the line of scrimmage, then turns to block back side; turn-back position is one yard behind line of scrimmage.

white area—Area on the field from the –10- to the +45-yard lines.

widen base—Stand with feet wider than shoulders.

wing—Running back aligns one yard behind the line of scrimmage and at least one yard outside the offensive tackle or tight end.

zone protection—Pass protectors blocking area, usually from outside shoulder of blocker to outside shoulder of teammate lined up to the inside.

CHAPTER 13

PERFORMANCE EVALUATION AND GRADING

Two types of evaluation are necessary to measure criteria essential for performance: evaluation of your own team and evaluation of the opposition. In-house evaluation includes analyzing individual, group, and team execution. Computers can be invaluable to any grading or evaluating procedure. Nonetheless, forms for recording information are still the most frequently used and preferred method of analysis.

Forms are a tool for collecting and classifying information. Data compiled on a well-conceived form allow for quick, complete bottom-line insights. A good form allows easy access and classification of raw observations. Evaluation and computing are the backbone for improvement and change.

The information in this section is not presented in any sequential or chronological order. The nature of each form, symbol, number, or letter used is only a suggestion for evaluating a particular element of offensive performance based on my experiences. What's important is that the method of recording is easy to calculate and understand so that the information gathered is accurate and useful.

Using Data

There is little value in compiling information unless it is used to improve your team's chances of success. Keep in mind the information collected is only as good as the person gathering it. Have qualified people collect and record all information.

When the quarterback reviews the information, he should expect to discover useful insights. Often formation changes or changes in motion or cadence can be used to overcome the defense if its tendencies can be predicted. When a coverage is tighter or looser, certain pass patterns match up better. Some alignments along the front invite a given play or encourage an offense to attack elsewhere. Knowing these things allows you to capitalize on the situation.

Information about the opponent, whether about defensive personnel or their system, enhances a quarterback's ability to perform. Self-evaluation also is positive with respect to measuring the status quo and comparing against goals. Grading and evaluating are necessary for gaining insight and progressing in ability.

There will always be a struggle on the way to improved performance, but it doesn't matter because that is part of getting better. The measuring of the struggle provides the thrust to achieve. In the 1990s, Kerry Collins, quarterback for the New York Giants, and Trent Dilfer, quarterback for the Baltimore Ravens, often admitted they had difficulty dominating in their positions. In 2001, both these players led their teams to the Super Bowl. Improved performance reflects knowing where you are as a player or a team first. Moving the bar up a notch, after honest assessment, becomes easy, logical, and productive.

Yesterday's performance is not good enough to win today. This philosophy is essential for a quarterback. There will be setbacks along the road, but they serve as a platform from which to grow. Who a person is now, this very minute, is only temporary. The major significance to grading and evaluating is to have a place from which to move forward. Measuring is sizing up what is pertinent to improving. Improving is what must happen to stay in a race and have an opportunity to win. The quarterback, more than anyone else, must rely on grading and performance evaluation to operate effectively.

Someone once said measuring is the only valid method to determine value, capacity, extent of range, dimension, or degree of anything. Thus for the field general, he must not only understand acquired essential information but apply it to his mission. Evaluation allows for the examination of the status quo, providing a picture from which to proceed. Without appraising, growth and development stagnate. A team's worst enemy is being satisfied!

There is no room on the football field for the rich, happy, and healthy—only performers. Performance is the doing part of being a quarterback. All the other stuff is incidental by comparison.

Offensive assessment must focus on the quarterback's efforts and the information he needs to successfully run the offense. It is imperative to measure his improvement and the production of the offense he leads, and gather information about the opposition. Much of this knowledge can be collected during practice or by viewing videotapes, though some data are recorded and used during the game itself.

The first form in this chapter is the game evaluation and individual performance form (table 13.1). This form has room to record information on play number, formation, play, grade, and comments.

■ Despite his struggles early in his career, Kerry Collins led the New York Giants to the Super Bowl in 2001.

Table 13.1 Game Evaluation and Individual Performance

Play number	Formation	Play	Grade	Comments

Play number refers to the order of play called, from the first play of the game to the last. Formation and play show the formation used and the number or name of the play. The evaluator can add a grade and comments in the last two columns.

The form is used to measure the quarterback's performance on each play. Symbols such as + (plus), – (minus), or NG (no grade) can be used in the grade column, or the letter grades A, B, C, D, or F can be used. The most popular manner of grading is to apply a number from 1 to 5 for each play, number 1 being the highest and 5 being the lowest. Regardless of the grading method, the coach and quarterback should jointly agree on the grade assessed. When and where this grading occurs is determined by what best serves the individual program.

The form can help a quarterback evaluate the number of times a specific play is called, from which formation the play is selected, and whether or not the play works (this is where the comments column can be most useful). The quarterback's grade on each play helps him understand how well he executed the plan.

Taking Notes and Grading

A coach can help a quarterback the most through stand-back observation during practice. The coach's insights should be written down and discussed with the signal caller after practice each day. Evaluating individual game performance is one thing, but examining the game plan and the various aspects of preparation is another. Ongoing observation during game week about the details of preparation is a must. This subjective analysis helps the quarterback understand the likelihood of success for a play or formation, how best to use personnel, the proper cadence, use of the field, and good communication.

On Tuesday and Wednesday of each game week, the coach and quarterback should evaluate the overall game plan for that week. To determine the worth or effectiveness of the preliminary plan, an assessment form is useful. The reverse side of a practice schedule card or form is a good place to note this data each day. This information can be transferred to an official form by Wednesday of each week.

Evaluation needs to appraise the formation and plays to be used. This includes quarterback actions, blocking patterns, line splits, use of motion, and personnel. This information should be explored in the context of the probable defensive structure the opponent will use.

Evaluating Coverage

Part of the signal caller's preparation is assessment of his opponent's coverage against his own passing plays. In the off-season or on the weekend before the next game, things may look good, but after a day or two of on-field execution against a scout team, the plan needs to be adjusted. Minor changes can smooth out problems and improve the strategy of the game plan. Sometimes plays or formations need to be thrown out, period.

Videotapes, the coach's observations, and the quarterback's input are sources that help to make the necessary determinations of details within the plan. It is a good idea to appraise two days of study to determine if there should be change, but sometimes one observation will do the trick. The earlier in the week this evaluation is done, the better, to allow for more repetition of the adjustments in the plan. Table 13.2 shows a sample pregame plan evaluation form.

The pregame plan evaluation form not only is valuable in making changes but also to keep as a record for use down the road. The same mistakes can be avoided if accurate records are kept. A computer can be used to store information for future reference. Evaluating the opposition this way helps quarterbacks develop a feel for how they can better execute their assignment, such as using a reverse pivot instead of fronting out, handing the ball off deeper rather than shallower, using a three-step drop instead of a five-step drop, or faking with one hand instead of two.

Spreading the coverage or reducing it with formations or motion also can change coverage, primary force, or who the contain man is. Some formations not only serve the play better but provide for more appropriate personnel matchups. Blocking patterns, too, often improve the success ratio of a play when careful analysis is compiled and applied.

Measuring Route Success

Every quarterback throws some pass routes better than others. This is true in practice as well as in games. The nature and ability of each signal caller often determine positive route selection. A quarterback with a strong arm may throw outs better than anything else. There are quarterbacks who have the ability to make the touch pass work with precision. The point is, whatever the

Table 13.2 Pregame Plan Evaluation

Opponent: _____   Date: _____

Formation	Play	Comments

quarterback's strongest skill, the system of play should incorporate this skill to the fullest.

Therefore, it is appropriate to determine lack of success when the quarterback throws certain routes. No one can improve unless he knows what to work on. Drills can be created to improve the skills of the quarterback if you can determine what needs to be improved. The form in table 13.3 is useful for recording this data.

This form should be used for ongoing examination of route production. It can be used for a season or a single game. It also can be used as a tool to examine routes thrown in practice.

Subjective evaluation of routes is often invalid, as coaches and quarterbacks tend to lose track of the whats, whens, and hows of specific routes. It's also human nature to recall a route the time it worked and forget the miscues. Consistency is what passing the football is all about. Recording and grading are the best ways to assess route success.

Evaluating the Opposition

Many other measuring processes aid in the evaluation of personnel, systems, and tendencies. A quarterback is better equipped to successfully perform if he has accurate information to help him deal with the challenges around him. Objective information outweighs subjective speculation or opinion when it comes to practical use of data. In no area is it more important to have essential facts than when dealing with the opposition. A quarterback must be able to understand all the defensive strengths and weaknesses of every team he competes against.

Pertinent data on the opponent are compiled on the coverages and fronts form (figure 13.1). This form allows for recognition of the defensive front and the coverage as it relates to the front. It reveals where and when the opposition uses these defenses. Most important of all, the coverages and fronts form classifies the defensive alignment against specific offensive formations. Superior and inferior opponent personnel can be color coded on this sheet for easy recognition. The quarterback can use the coverages and fronts form as a scouting or videotape breakdown tool.

Table 13.3   Pass Routes and Production

Route	Hash	Cover	Grade	Comments

Figure 13.1

Coverages and fronts

Opponent _____ Date _____

---

40 base

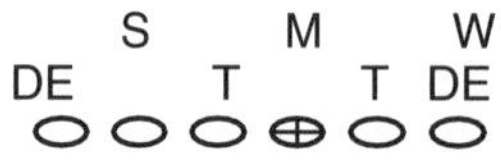

```
     S    M    W
DE     T    T    DE
  ○  ○  ○  ⊕  ○  ○
```

Down and distance _____ Yardline _____
Hash _____
Formation _____
Cover _____

---

40 strong

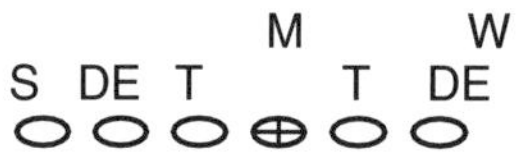

```
          M    W
S  DE  T       T   DE
  ○  ○  ○  ⊕  ○  ○
```

Down and distance _____ Yardline _____
Hash _____
Formation _____
Cover _____

---

40 weak

```
     S    M    W
DE     T       T   DE
  ○  ○  ○  ⊕  ○  ○
```

Down and distance _____ Yardline _____
Hash _____
Formation _____
Cover _____

---

40 stack

```
          M    W
S  DE   T      T  DE
  ○  ○  ○  ⊕  ○  ○
```

Down and distance _____ Yardline _____
Hash _____
Formation _____
Cover _____

---

62 goal line

```
    FS   M    W
 S  DE    T    T   DE  SS
  ○  ○  ○  ⊕  ○  ○  ○
```

Down and distance _____ Yardline _____
Hash _____
Formation _____
Cover _____

---

50 straight

```
        M    W
DE   T    N      T  DE
  ○  ○  ○  ⊕  ○  ○
```

Down and distance _____ Yardline _____
Hash _____
Formation _____
Cover _____

---

50 slide

```
       M    W
DE  T    N     T   DE
  ○  ○  ○  ⊕  ○  ○
```

Down and distance _____ Yardline _____
Hash _____
Formation __ _____
Cover _____

---

50 split

```
          M  W
 S  DE  T       T  DE
  ○  ○  ○  ⊕  ○  ○
```

Down and distance _____ Yardline _____
Hash _____
Formation _____
Cover _____

Coverages and fronts form.

Overview Form

The coverages and fronts form supplies a broad look for the quarterback of these two concerns. A more detailed comprehensive analysis of the opponent's defense is found on the overview form (figure 13.2). The overview form supplies a breakdown of the opponent. It categorizes the most pertinent data for the quarterback with respect to the situations he will face in the contest.

A computer can help sort out large amounts of data. Information from videotapes and scouting reports can be fed into a computer for the computer to separate, itemize, and summarize. The goal is to produce a visual portrait of the opposition's defensive personality and tendencies. Total insights into how a team thinks as well as performs are dissected. Here are sample report topics:

- Front variation percentages overall
- Linebacker alignment against offensive formation
- Coverage from hash to formations and field position
- Motion adjustments
- Third-and-long (over six yards) front/cover
- Third-and-short (under two yards) front/cover
- Red zone (+20) front/cover
- Line stunts from which alignment
- Linebacker blitzes from which alignments and coverage
- Front late changes in shades

The overview analysis also can provide the quarterback with the success ratio of other teams that have already played this opponent, not only their overall success, but the specifics (for example, where running attacks succeeded, how passing attacks defeated coverages). All this information can be illustrated with bar graphs, percentage breakdowns, and graphic charts. These visual aids are dramatic and easy to digest.

The worth of this information is obviously invaluable to quarterback preparation. A quarterback can understand vulnerabilities and strengths of the opposition if he absorbs the information available via the overview breakdown summaries. Following are some of the charts that computer technology can spit out when given appropriate data. Examples of percentage evaluations follow.

Figure 13.2

Percentage evaluations

Front percentage		Linebacker alignment	
Front percentage	Percent	Linebacker	Percent
30		Straight	
40		Stack	
50		Walk up	
60		Eagle	
		Wide	

Coverage by field position				Coverage with motion			
Formation	Hash	Yardline	Coverage	Formation	Hash	Yardline	Coverage
Pro				Flanker			
Slot				Slot			
Slot open				Wing			
Trips				Running			
Tight				back			
Open							
Bunch							

Third and long				Third and short			
Hash	Front	Cover	Percent	Hash	Front	Cover	Percent
Left				Left			
Middle				Middle			
Right				Right			

Red zone				Red zone line variations and stunts			
Down and distance	Front	Cover	Percent	Down and distance	Front	Cover	Percent
1 and 10				1			
2 and 7+				2 and long			
2 and 4-6				2 and medium			
2 and 1-2				2 and short			
3 and 5+				3 and long			
3 and 2-4				3 and short			
3 and 1-3				4			

Linebacker blitzes			Front late changes and shades		
Down and distance	Linebacker	Percent	Down and distance	Shift to	Percent
1 and 10			30		
2 and 7+			40 straight		
2 and 4-6			40 weak		
2 and 1-3			40 strong		
3 and 7+			40 stack		
3 and 4-6			50 straight		
3 and 1-3			50 weak		
4 and 3+			50 strong		
			60 straight		
			60 weak		
			60 strong		

Overview form.

Other information such as front slanting personnel substitution, spacing/alignment within coverage, or linebacker drops can be drawn from the data. This knowledge can be noted on a defensive overview form.

Attacking Zone Coverage

The normal zone responsibilities form (figure 13.3) zeroes in strictly on a team's coverage responsibility. A quarterback can lean heavily on the information from this form as he prepares the passing package to be used for a game. This form breaks down the areas of the football field into zones in which the quarterback's pass offense might best operate. By identifying the areas and who defensively will occupy them, a quarterback can better understand how his pass offense will function against any zone coverage.

Short zones should feature pass plays such as delays, slants, quick outs, hitches, drags, short curls, two-man combos, running back routes, and screens. A lot of passes thrown are in the intermediate area of the coverage, where deeper curls, outs, crossing patterns, stops, seams, hooks, and angle routes head the list of plays that should have good results. Attacking the deeper zones successfully requires pass patterns such as posts, flags, deep crosses, verticals, fades, and combo routes. In understanding the makeup of patterns and the zone to be attacked, the quarterback isolates and simplifies the objective of the pass play. When a quarterback knows the area breakdowns, it is easier for him to pick up the appropriate defender for keying within that zone. For example, he might key the outside weak linebacker or weak corner when throwing to the weak-side flat.

In area coverage, breakdown responsibility is almost always as seen in table 13.4, depending on the type of zone coverage.

Overcoming Man Coverage

Unlike zone coverage, man-to-man pits one defender against one offensive player from the snap, with the idea of switching coverage, from covering an area to defending against a person. A man-to-man defense is only as good as its least capable defender. Man coverage allows for blitz or pressure defense because linebackers are not always assigned an area to defend, as they are in zone coverage.

Figure 13.3

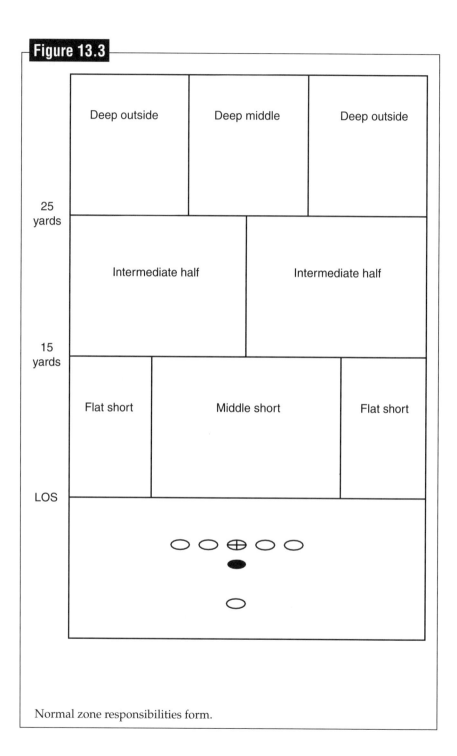

Normal zone responsibilities form.

Table 13.4   Area Coverage Breakdowns

Short zones	Intermediate zones	Middle deep
Weak side—weak line-backer or corner	Weak side—weak corner or safety	Deep outside—corner or safety
Middle—middle backer	Strong side—strong corner or safety	Deep middle—corner or safety
Strong side—strong backer, strong safety, or strong corner		

Confronted with man coverage, the quarterback's keys no longer apply. Instead, the quarterback relies more on getting the desired matchups and timing his passes. Good receiver route technique becomes extremely important for success against any form of man coverage. Isolation of a receiver and his relationship to another receiver is also necessary for positive production versus man-to-man coverage. There are two basic types of man coverages: man lock and man free (figure 13.4).

In man coverage, linebackers are sometimes assigned to cover running backs. Man cover varies as to which linebacker covers which back. Generally a linebacker locks on to the back that releases to his side, called *area man coverage*. Normally the assignment, whether lock or area man coverage, is decided on a game-to-game basis.

Before the snap, the quarterback should attempt to determine whether the coverage is zone or man. Stance, depth, body alignment, and position relationship of defensive backs provide clues. The quarterback's knowledge of the opponent's tendencies and philosophy also help him determine the likelihood of zone or man cover.

Sizing Up Defensive Personnel

A quarterback who knows the strength of the opposition's personnel is miles ahead of the guy that doesn't. The quarterback needs to know who the best pass rushers, run defenders, and coverage players are. Plays can be designed accordingly to take advantage of these situations. Play selection during a contest should consider the quality of the opponent's players.

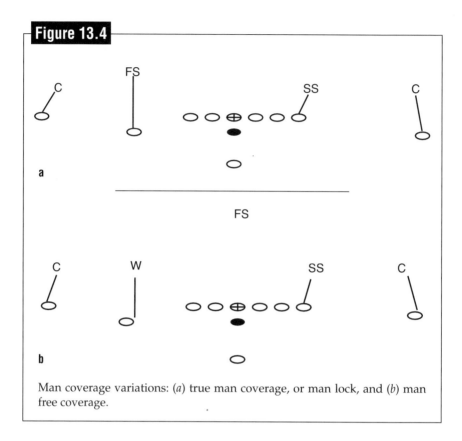

Figure 13.4

Man coverage variations: (*a*) true man coverage, or man lock, and (*b*) man free coverage.

A proven method to determine the ability level of an opponent is to measure each player on a play-by-play basis. A tool that can be used to accomplish this is the player evaluation form (table 13.5). This form measures a player's performance level in two categories: speed, or quickness, and ability. Using a scale of 1 to 5 (usually 1 is the highest and 5 the lowest), evaluators can rank/classify an athlete according to his potential effectiveness and talent level.

Every defense has its favorite alignments and tendencies. The quarterback who is aware of this information can make the best decision possible to exploit who he is playing. The most commonly used fronts are 30, 40, and 50 (figure 13.5). All these alignments have adjustments within the front such as strong, slide, or weak. Shades on offensive linemen always strengthen or weaken these base alignments.

Table 13.5   Player Evaluation Form

Player number	Name	Height	Weight	Speed/quickness	Ability	Year

Figure 13.5

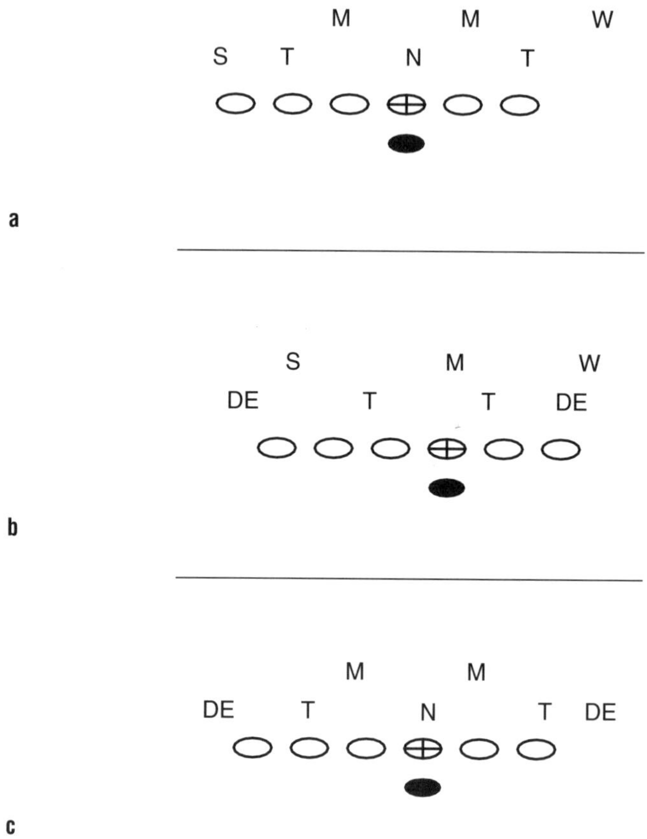

Frequently used fronts: (*a*) 30, (*b*) 40, and (*c*) 50.

Evaluation on Game Day

As a contest goes along, it is valuable to assess what the defense is doing. The checks, changes, and specific alignments a defense exhibits provide an ongoing picture of the challenge at hand. The game day offense versus defense chart (table 13.6) gives immediate data that the quarterback needs to perform properly. This chart should be kept on the sideline, even if the person on the boundary needs help from the press box. The quarterback can scan the information between series or drives, allowing him to keep the pulse of his offense.

Specific Defensive Tendency Form

Within the coverages and fronts tendencies against a formation, there is additional information that can serve to identify opponent strategy. The data from the specific defensive tendency chart (figure 13.6) primarily pinpoints field position. This information is important for a quarterback because it gives him the perception of how the defense will defend in specific areas of the field. Most teams' defensive philosophy changes as an offense goes up the playing field.

Mohammed Ali, former world heavyweight champion, used to say, "I am the greatest," on a regular basis. Many would agree with him, and he was surely unique in many ways. Whether he could wear a large "S" on his chest legitimately or not, who knows? The point is that most quarterbacks are not the greatest but need day-to-day progress to even have a chance to perform near their potential. All improvement for an offense and a quarterback is stimulated by measurement. The worth of honest evaluation cannot be stressed enough. Getting better is directly connected to analyzing what has taken place. Unless a quarterback knows where he is, he can't know where he or his team is going. Grading and evaluating are part of the learning and improvement process, and are vital tools for the development of every quarterback.

Table 13.6   Game Day Offense Versus Defense Chart

Number	Hash	Formation	Play	Gain	Comments

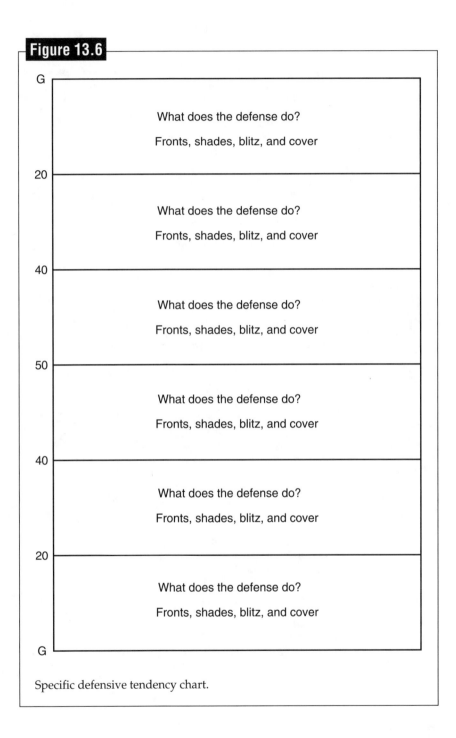

Figure 13.6

Specific defensive tendency chart.

CHAPTER 14

OFF-SEASON DEVELOPMENT

Unfortunately, many quarterbacks become casualties of their position. A primary reason for failure is off-season development or, rather, lack of it. Work done in the period between one season and another is critical for a quarterback. Refinement of skills and fitness, usually the main objective in the off-season, is accelerated for the quarterback who is committed to excellence. There is no hope for the satisfied quarterback.

One of football's greatest coaches, Vince Lombardi, preached, "The harder you work, the harder it is to surrender!" All activity in the months following the season can be classified as either physical or mental development. For the signal caller, this activity is an investment in himself.

Physical Gains

Physical gains come in four areas of concentration: flexibility, quickness, strength, and passing velocity and accuracy. It has been proved time and time again that durability correlates to being physically fit. No position in football is exposed to a greater risk of injury than the quarterback. A quarterback who faithfully follows a carefully planned training program in the off-season is bound to be more durable and therefore less prone to injury.

Flexibility

A quarterback needs maximum flexibility to excel. Playing quarterback is centered around physical movement. Flexibility helps the quarterback execute his responsibilities on the field without causing serious damage to his joints or ligaments. Flexibility work can be divided into upper-body and lower-body work. Stretching to improve range of motion can precede strength or quickness workouts, but there is more gain if stretching is done after a physical workout.

An upper-body flexibility workout should include the following exercises:

- Pull arms across body—pull left arm across to the right side, then the right arm across to the left side.
- Roll shoulders and arms in a circular direction.
- Rotate neck in a circular direction.
- Reach overhead or bend at the waist and let arms hang toward the floor.

Lower-body flexibility exercises should include the following:

- Twist hips in a circular direction, then to the left and right.
- While standing, spread legs wide apart and reach through with the arms.
- While standing, spread legs wide apart, then bring head to one knee and then the other.
- Straddle split on the ground and lean the body forward.
- From a sitting position, with the feet wide apart, grab and hold the toes.

All stretches should be held for 10 seconds. Before stretching, the athlete should jog for three minutes unless his muscles are completely warm from activity.

Quickness Work

Quickness for the quarterback is imperative for drops, spills and scrambles, sprint outs, options, and slides in the pocket. These aspects of quarterbacking can be improved through off-season workouts. A quarterback should commit about 20 minutes, three days a week in the off-season to various forms of quickness work after warming up. Quickness activities include the following:

- Jump rope for speed (15-second bursts), 6 times.
- Hop over a cone for speed (15-second bursts), 6 times.
- Backpedal for speed for 10 yards, 6 times.
- Carioca for 10 yards, 6 times.
- Run short sprints for 20 yards, 10 times.
- Run stairs, run in sand, or run in place for five minutes.

Form running as part of the warm up is also good for development and technique. There are many speed programs that emphasize running fundamentals and accelerate development even further.

© The Sporting Image/Kirby Lee

■ Off-season training is crucial for a quarterback who wants to play at a higher level. An elite quarterback must have tremendous strength, flexibility, quickness, and accuracy.

Zigzag or shuttle running is another phase of speed work that helps overall quickness. Change of direction drills contribute even more to the improvement of foot speed. The following change of direction drill serves as a good example for quick feet development. To execute this drill, the coach stands 10 yards from the player, pointing with his arm to the direction desired. The player reacts accordingly at full speed. Several people can be placed in line, from left to right, and directed at the same time in this drill.

It is best if the quarterback does this training on grass while wearing good shoes with traction. It is better to work out when it's warm than when it's cold. The quarterback should keep records on his workouts and be timed periodically for motivation and to show improvement. For a quarterback, slow feet are a killer! Quick feet can be a quarterback's greatest asset.

Strength Training

Strength aids a quarterback in the areas of durability, throwing, and movement. A quarterback is not after big muscle definition but rather a well-balanced, overall strong body. Lighter weights, with increased repetitions, are the right formula. A lifting program for a quarterback should include the following:

- Speed squats 8 × 3 (eight sets of three repetitions)
- Deadlifts 3 × 10
- Pulldowns 3 × 10
- Bench presses 3 × 6
- Push presses 2 × 8
- Incline presses 3 × 12
- Shoulder raises 3 × 10
- Upright rows 3 × 10
- Pullovers 3 × 10
- Front deltoid raises 3 × 10
- Straight-leg deadlifts 3 × 10
- Hang cleans 3 × 8
- Calf raises 3 × 10
- Shoulder presses 3 × 10
- Back rows 3 × 10
- Lateral shoulder raises 3 × 12

- Rear deltoid raises 3 × 12
- Hip extensions 2 × 8

For a six day per week lifting program, three days should be spent on upper body, three days on lower body. The six days a week program provides ideal growth and development. Remember, maxing out or heavy lifting is not necessarily good and should not be the goal of a quarterback's off-season strength work. Lighter weight and more reps generally will help the quarterback become a more functional player.

Passing Velocity and Accuracy

As discussed in chapter 7, passing the football correctly requires precise execution. This skill can be developed in the off-season. The first step is to set specific objectives for the end result and for each workout. Goals should focus on two objectives: velocity and accuracy. Workouts need to zero in on either or both aspects of passing development. A few specific drills for cultivating these passing elements are presented in chapter 7.

Velocity drills include the throws from knees drill and wrong foot forward drill described in chapter 7. Both of these activities should be done after the quarterback warms up his arm by playing catch. For the drills, the quarterback sets up 10 yards from the receiver. Balls should be thrown as hard as possible from the natural throwing position, about numbers high. These two drills remove body momentum from the throw, placing stress on the arm.

Drills that improve and fine-tune passing feature follow-through action. One-knee drills and one-step throwing drills best improve accuracy in passing. The one-knee drill puts the quarterback in an ideal throwing position, allowing full hip rotation, shoulder leverage, and complete range of motion for the arm. As in the velocity throwing drills, accuracy drills should begin with the football in both hands at the base of the numbers. From this position, the nonthrowing hand pushes the football up in the natural throwing action. The ball comes down and through in front of the body, with the fingers coming off the ball in order from little finger to index finger. The index finger pushes the ball in the direction desired. As in velocity drills, the quarterback should be 10 yards away from the receiver. The pigskin should be thrown as hard as possible. After the football leaves the throwing hand, the arm (if the action is correct) will move naturally toward the ground, with the palm rotating out and down. If the ball doesn't hit a predetermined spot on the receiver, adjustment in the arm action is needed or the ball needs to be adjusted in the palm. Refer to chapter 7 for more insight into throwing mechanics.

Mental Work

Mental training is even more demanding in the off-season than physical training. Mental adaptation is extremely complex and involved. The amount of improvement to be gained between seasons is enormous. The mental progression can be divided into five categories:

1. In-depth knowledge of the next season's opponents
2. Magnified examination of last season's team performance
3. A play-by-play focused look at all previous plays, games, or practices
4. Meeting with position coaches about their players and system technology
5. Study of other quarterbacks to see better techniques

Time at least every other day should be set aside for working on the quarterback's mental preparation. One or two hours for this purpose is reasonable to expect from a hungry-for-improvement quarterback. The best way to ensure this complete study for a quarterback is to map out a calendar listing the what, when, and how of accomplishing his off-season goals. There will be limited position development for a quarterback unless he makes getting better a top priority in his life.

Don't forget, great quarterbacks can be developed. Work and study are the ingredients to improvement. Time and effort always pay big dividends. Without intense off-season effort, a quarterback lets his team down and falls short of realizing his own potential. Potential, remember, is all that is left when there is a lack of application. The football world is full of guys with potential. All potential without application does is allow you to come in second. In football, coming in second equals losing. If a person wants to be bigger, stronger, faster, or better, there is only one way. Accomplishing and meeting these goals takes place from January through August in off-season development.

A motto every quarterback should adopt is you can always play better. The formula for improvement was coined more than 200 years ago by Benjamin Franklin when he said, "There are no gains without pains." Achievement is the by-product of work—that's how it is.

On the bulletin board in the team room at the University of Montana a sign reads, "One thing today, another tomorrow." Where a quarterback is today is not where he will be tomorrow if he desires change. Tomorrow for the quarterback is now. Now means off-season commitment.

The primary goal for a quarterback in the off-season is to get good at something. Perfecting a skill he can become known for should be the driving, motivating force for a signal caller. It's not that improvement overall can't be made because it can. But being the best at a specific type of pass or running play builds confidence. The end result is a quarterback who has something he can turn to when needed. All great quarterbacks are exceptional at one skill or another. The off-season is where such perfection can be acquired.

The old adage "When you're good, you're good. When you're not, you're not" is only partly true, as there is usually room for improvement. Almost all "should have been" or "could have been" quarterbacks are tied to lack of commitment in the off-season.

Ernest Hemingway said, "The only way to get better at writing is to write." The same applies to quarterbacks; the only way to get better is to quarterback. Repetition and studying technique are the recipe for improvement. It is during the off-season that major steps toward mastery of needed skills, both mental and physical, are taken. The motivation for off-season development is expressed best in the often-used phrase "The possible I can do now; the impossible takes a little longer." For each quarterback, the possibility of improvement is real; the choice belongs to him.

Self-sacrifice needs to be a characteristic of every quarterback. Getting better is all about work. For the signal caller, this translates to 12 months of systematic, hard-core physical and mental commitment.

Thomas Jefferson once said, "I am a great believer in luck, and I find the harder I work, the more I have of it." Former President Jefferson's ideology parallels that of a 20th-century president, Franklin D. Roosevelt. In a speech to the American people, Mr. Roosevelt stated that happiness lies in the joy of achievement and the thrill of creative effort. Both these great leaders knew well that

■ Improvement in the off-season is possible for the quarterback who puts in the work.

© Newsport Photography

without a work ethic people stand still. Development for the quarterback depends on what he is willing to do. Growth is first a plan, but then it comes down to working that plan to the maximum. The off-season provides a quarterback's best opportunity to do just that.

The off-season gives a signal caller not only time to make physical and mental gains but to influence teammate commitment. There is no better form of leadership than that of doing what others expect and doing it enthusiastically. Because off-season training is less formal, the quarterback can work with teammates in a more casual manner, which often helps relationships grow and prosper. The off-season invites refined development, as concentration can be on personal gains rather than readying for opponents.

Keep in mind that there are many kinds of development techniques that can take place in the off-season; going over the playbook, evaluating defensive tendencies of upcoming opponents, and evaluating your own teammates and offensive strengths are but a few. Last, there are passing camps, passing leagues, and clinics where quarterbacks have an opportunity to grow and develop. These off-season activities go on every summer in every state in the United States. Improvement is tied to this type of commitment. Potential is just that unless change by way of hard work makes it a reality.

An old motivational statement this coach has used for years to emphasize a point is offered here as advice to quarterbacks in terms of off-season work: Get after it! This advice is extended to past quarterbacks and to those who coach them, as well.

About the Author

Don Read is perhaps best known for his ability to overcome obstacles and to produce winning football teams that were led by outstanding quarterbacks. He began his head coaching career in 1962 in the high school ranks at Petaluma, California, where he took a downtrodden program to four straight championships. During this time, he was chosen NCAA Coach of the Year twice.

Subsequent coaching stops include Humboldt State University, two stints at Portland State University, the University of Oregon, Oregon Institute of Technology, and the University of Montana, where he coached from 1986 until he retired in 1996 after leading the Grizzlies to their first-ever national championship in 1995. With each new job, Read was given the daunting task of turning around a losing program. Read met that challenge each and every time with success on the field and admiration from his colleagues as well as his players.

Winning more than 70 percent of his games, Don Read ranks among the nation's most successful coaches. He has coached 49 players who have gone on to play in professional football, including Jim Costello, Tim Von Dulm, June Jones, Dan Fouts, and Norv Turner. Read has been the Western Football Conference, Evergreen Conference, and Big Sky Conference Coach of the Year, NCAA Regional Coach of the Year twice, and National Coach of the Year.

Don Read is a highly sought after clinician who has written scores of articles on coaching and the quarterback position. Read is a Christian and dedicated family man and lives in Colorado with his wife Lois.

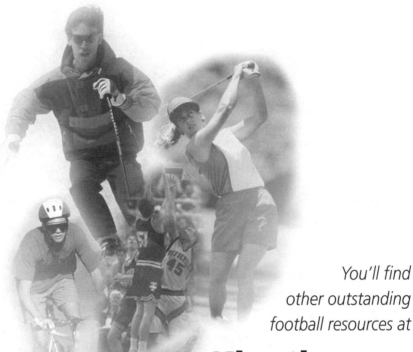

*You'll find
other outstanding
football resources at*

www.HumanKinetics.com

In the U.S. call

1-800-747-4457

Australia 08 8277 1555
Canada 800-465-7301
Europe .... +44 (0) 113 255 5665
New Zealand 09-523-3462

HUMAN KINETICS
The Premier Publisher for Sports and Fitness
P.O. Box 5076 • Champaign, IL 61825-5076 USA